The Gospel of Matthew

PROCLAIMING THE NEW TESTAMENT

The Gospel
of Matthew

by
Herschel H. Hobbs

BAKER BOOK HOUSE
Grand Rapids 6, Michigan
1961

Library of Congress Catalog Card Number 61-10006

PHOTOLITHOPRINTED BY CUSHING ~ MALLOY, INC.
ANN ARBOR, MICHIGAN, UNITED STATES OF AMERICA
1961

DEDICATED

to

JERRY AND LYNNE

with the prayer that their lives together
may be used in the service of the King.

Editor's Foreword

In the series, Proclaiming the New Testament, an attempt is made to provide homiletical comments and ideas. The busy pastor needs to spend time in meditation if he is to offer the bread of life to his people. One of the best known methods of Bible study is to work through one book of the Bible at a time. This gives depth as well as breadth. It provides for the preaching of the whole counsel of God and not just a part of that revelation. As truth must reach people in various stages of growth and at different levels of reception, so there must be variety of communication.

The intention of this series is to stimulate men in the ministry to more definite study. Believing that the first rule of homiletics is to read and study the actual text of Scripture, this method brings ideas and suggestion. Here illustrations are limited as the individual should find his own as he reads or mingles with people, and as he is open to all the winds of God. No pastor can lead his people to a level of thought and spiritual experience higher than the one he occupies. God will not honor lazy men or men who imagine the Holy Spirit should prompt alone. God has given us a mind to use, a heart to love, a spirit to pray, and a will to study.

These results are possible from this approach. *One,* the pastor and student will find suggestive ideas. As Charles H. Spurgeon said of William Gurnall (1616-79), a Puritan, "I have found his work the best thought-breeder in all our library. I should think more discourses have been suggested by it than by any other. I have often resorted to it when my own fire has been burning low...." *Two,* the user will see how to study an entire book of the Bible for preaching values. *Three,* the man of God will be encouraged to begin the study of the Bible book for himself and find by this method other treasures of homiletical insight.

While using the King James or Authorized Version, the student should compare with all other versions and translations as well as the original text when available.

Many and varied are the commentaries available for the profit of the preacher. These include the following:

I. *Critical.* This deals with the text in the light of biblical criticism, seeking to apply historical principles and a rational approach to the text, e.g., *The International Critical Commentary, The Moffatt New Testament Commentary, The Expositor's Greek Testament,* and the commentaries of H. A. W. Meyer, and Keil and Delitsch.

II. *Exegetical.* This seeks to lead out the exact meaning of the text in terms of the words and idioms in the light of their background and use originally, e.g., *The Westminster Commentaries, The New International Commentary on the New Testament, The Evangelical Commentary on the New Testament,* and the commentaries of R. C. H. Lenski, J. P. Lange, and W. Hendriksen.

III. *Expository.* This expounds and applies the dominant theme of each section or unit in the light of history and with relevance to the present, e.g., *The Expositor's Bible, The Interpreter's Bible, Calvin's Commentaries, The Pulpit Commentary,* and *An American Commentary on the New Testament.*

IV. *Devotional.* This brings out the inner sense or the spiritual essence as applied to the soul in meditation. Here is the stimulus to the spiritual life of the believer, e.g., *A Devotional Commentary,* and Matthew Henry's *Commentary on the Whole Bible.*

The present type of book is neither a Bible study book nor a book of outlines. It is not a commentary as the above. We seek to encourage the preacher to engage in the reading and studying of the book to find the homiletical units. As "the servant of the Word" let him work toward this ideal:

the Historical setting,
the Expository meaning,
the Doctrinal value,
the Practical aim,
the Homiletical form

The First Presbyterian Church
of Seattle, Washington

Ralph G. Turnbull
General Editor

Introduction

The Gospel of Matthew is the Gospel of the King. It was possibly written to convince the Jews that Jesus was their Messiah, the long-awaited King. As such it makes much use of Old Testament prophecy.

This volume is written on the assumption that this Gospel was written by Matthew or Levi, the publican. According to Papias, as quoted by Eusebius, Matthew wrote the *Logia,* a record of Jesus, in Hebrew or Aramaic. Some see this Gospel as a Greek translation of the *Logia.* However, there is no reason why Matthew could not have written both. As a publican Matthew was accustomed to keeping records. One can almost see him taking notes as Jesus taught. Thus we are not surprised to see the great detail with which Matthew reports the teachings of Jesus: the Sermon on the Mount (Chapters 5-7) ; the parables (Chapter 13) ; the denunciation of the Pharisees (Chapter 23) ; and the eschatalogical discourse (Chapters 24-25) .

The date of this Gospel calls for attention. Because of the detailed description of the destruction of Jerusalem (Chapter 24) , some would date it after A.D. 70. But if one accepts the deity of Jesus Christ, there is no reason why it could not have been written prior to that time. Thus it becomes prophecy of the event rather than a history of it. Matthew, like Luke, makes much use of the material found in Mark. Therefore it must have been written after Mark. It could have been written either before or after Luke. However, Matthew shows no reliance upon Luke's account. This may or may not show the priority of Matthew over Luke. The order of the two is not certain, nor is it of great importance. Mark's Gospel probably was written as early as A.D. 50. If so, then sometime between A.D. 55-60 would serve as a probable date for Matthew.

The purpose of this volume is quite plain. It is neither a commentary nor an exposition. It is not a book of sermons. Rather it is intended as an aid in sermon or devotional preparation. With it goes the prayer that it may save busy servants of the King many precious hours of research, and that through them its ministry may be enhanced beyond measure.

Herschel H. Hobbs

Pastor's Study
First Baptist Church
Oklahoma City, Oklahoma
February 1961

Contents

Matthew 1

THE SAVIOURHOOD OF JESUS CHRIST

1:21 "And she shall bring forth a son, and thou shalt call his name JESUS: for he shall save his people from their sins."

I. HISTORICAL SETTING. This is the climax of the genealogical introduction to The Gospel of Matthew. The Jews placed great importance upon their genealogical line, which was traced through the line of the father. Since Matthew is writing primarily for the Jews to prove the Messianic lineage of Jesus, he traces it through the Davidic line of Joseph. But since both Joseph and Mary were of the line of David, the genealogy is a true one with the exception of Jesus' immediate parentage. Matthew is careful to point out that Joseph is not the actual, but legal, father of Jesus (1:16-25). Luke writing for Gentile readers, gives the actual genealogy of Jesus through Mary.

II. EXPOSITORY MEANING. The words "bring forth" (cf. 1:23) render a Greek verb meaning "to give birth." Its noun form is "child." Literally, "she shall child a son." The verbs "bring forth," "call," and "save" are all prophetic future tenses. "JESUS" is the Greek equivalent of the Hebrew word *Joshua* or *Jehoshuah* (cf. English, John; and Spanish, Juan), meaning "Jehovah is helper," "Help of Jehovah," or "Jehovah is salvation." "He" in Greek is emphatic, "He Himself." "Save" means to preserve or deliver. It sometimes refers to physical danger (8:25), disease (9:21-22), or death (24:22). More often it is related to spiritual salvation. "People" could refer to Israel, or to all people (Luke 2:10). Probably it refers to the spiritual Israel (Rom. 9:25-26, 30). He will save all who trust in Him. "Sins" renders a Greek word meaning "to miss the mark" or target, the target being the will and righteousness of God. Literally, "He Himself, and no other, shall save

His people from their sins." "From" translates the Greek preposition *apo,* away from. Jesus will save away from sins. They will be cast away from and out of sight (cf. Ps. 103:12; Isa. 38:17). Although Matthew wrote primarily for Jewish readers, the scope of Jesus' saving ministry includes the whole world (John 3:16).

III. DOCTRINAL VALUE. The major doctrine involved is the person and work of Jesus Christ. This doctrine also includes the virgin birth, the nature of sin, the crucifixion, resurrection, ascension, and the continued intercession of the Son of God. Study Luke's account of the birth of Jesus and the prophetic utterances in Isaiah 7:10-16; 9:1-7. Note also Acts 4:10-12 and Philippians 2:5-11.

IV. PRACTICAL AIM. To show that God has moved in history to redeem a lost world. This salvation is not military, political, or social. It is spiritual. Of his own accord man is unable to save himself. It required a mighty act from God. But man is saved as an individual. What is God's part? What is man's role in his salvation?

V. HOMILETICAL FORM

Theme: "The Saviourhood of Jesus Christ."

Introduction: Joseph was betrothed to Mary, which in Jewish life was little short of marriage. Before they came together in marriage Joseph discovered that Mary was with child. As a *just* man, living according to the law, Joseph felt that he was unable to enter into marriage with Mary. But because of his love for her he was not *willing* to embarrass her publicly. Therefore he *wished* to divorce her privately, which was his right under the law. While Joseph was in this state of mind, an angel of the Lord revealed in a dream the true nature of Mary's condition. The climax of this revelation is the key verse of the chapter in which is expressed the redemptive purpose of God. Herein we find the Saviour identified; the Saviour specified; the salvation classified.

A. *The Saviour Identified* — "Thou shalt call his name JESUS." This is the focal point of prophecy. God had made promises concerning the "seed" of the woman (Gen. 3:15) and the "seed" of Abraham (Gen. 22:18; Gal. 3:16). Through Isaiah He had promised a child born of a virgin (7:15; 9:6-7). The hopes of Israel, even of the entire world, centered upon these promises.

To Joseph, therefore, the evangel was given that God was moving in history for His eternal redemptive purpose. The child of promise shall be called "Jesus," meaning *Jehovah is salvation.*

Conceived of the Holy Spirit, He is God. Born of the virgin Mary, He is man. He is the God-man. Only thus could the person of God find interplay with the person of man. Christ, the anointed one, is His eternal name. Jesus, help of Jehovah, is His human name. He is Emmanuel, God with us, to help and to save.

Jesus is the Greek equivalent of the Hebrew Joshua. Like Joshua, the prophet, He prophesies, "The Lord will do great wonders among you" (Josh. 3:5). Like Joshua, the priest, He will deliver the captives from their bondage (Ezra 2:2). Like Joshua, the ruler, He will lead into the salvation promised of the Lord (Josh. 1:6). He is Prophet, Priest, and King!

B. *The Saviour Specified* — "He [himself] shall save." Matthew's quotation (1:22-23) refers back to Isaiah 7-9. Ahaz sought deliverance by military alliances, soothsayers, and wizards. He refused to trust in the promises of Jehovah. In the time preceding and following the first century, the Jews trusted in many false military "messiahs" to their own hurt and loss. Monuments and inscriptions abound in the title "Saviour" applied to the Caesars and others. Even the Gentiles looked for a saviour of their own making and choosing. God says that Jesus himself shall save. He is set apart and above all others.

After two thousand years man still looks for salvation from his own ranks. The frustration seen on every hand is the direct result of such futile hopes. Amid the desolate cries of every failure of man may be heard the still small voice of God, "JESUS ... he [himself] shall save" (cf. Acts 4:10-12).

C. *The Salvation Classified* — "He shall save his people from their sins." This salvation is a deliverance. The Jews thought in terms of military and political deliverance. The apochryphal writing of the Jews just before and during the lifetime of Jesus pictured the Messiah as a military conqueror. Under him Israel would drive out the Romans, and from Jerusalem would rule the world (cf. Luke 24:21; Acts 1:6). Such a deliverance included only the Jews.

From the New Testament it is clear that "his people" involves all men. "God so loved the world [inhabited earth] . . . whosoever believeth . . ." (John 3:16; cf. John 10:16). The Jews regarded themselves alone as God's people. But Paul is careful to point out that not all citizens of political Israel were God's people (Rom. 9:6-13; Rom. 11:1-4; cf. Matt. 3:7-9). Furthermore those who were formerly not a people shall be called the people of God (I Peter 2:9-10; cf. of Rom. 11:17-32). This new relationship is not genetical or political, but spiritual.

This is the scope of the New Testament. It is involved in Matthew 1:21.

Matthew 2

THE RECEPTION OF THE KING

2:1. "Now when Jesus was born in Bethlehem of Judaea in the days of Herod the king, behold, there came wise men from the east to Jerusalem,"

2:2. "Saying, Where is he that is born King of the Jews? for we have seen his star in the east, and are come to worship him."

2:3. "When Herod the king had heard these things, he was troubled, and all Jerusalem with him."

I. HISTORICAL SETTING. The time is 6 or 5 B.C. Matthew dates Jesus' birth in the closing years of the reign of Herod the Great who died in 4 B.C. A. T. Robertson gives eight reasons for the above date of Jesus' birth (*A Harmony of the Gospels,* Broadman, Nashville) : death of Herod, slaughter of the infants, the star, language of Luke 2:14 about "peace on earth," beginning of the ministry of John the Baptist, beginning of the ministry of Jesus, building of the temple, Roman census of Luke 2:1 f.

The place is Bethlehem of Judaea, near Jerusalem, not the Bethlehem near Nazareth mentioned by Josephus (*Antiquities* XIX. 15) . Bethlehem was the home of David. Being of his lineage Joseph and Mary went there to enroll for taxation (Luke 2:1-4) .

The wise men may have come from Babylon, Persia, Parthia, Arabia, or elsewhere, probably from somewhere east of Palestine. The number "three" is legendary, inferred from the number of gifts brought. Legend also names them Caspar, Balthasar, and Melchoir; and suggests that they represent Shem, Ham, and Japheth. They were probably astrologers.

II. EXPOSITORY MEANING

Matt. 1:1. "When" is not in the Greek. The form is a genitive absolute construction. Literally it reads, "Now about the birth of Jesus." "Was born" is a passive participle of the verb *to beget*. "In the days of Herod" is an indefinite time referring to the evil time in which Jesus was born. *Herod* was the son of Antipater, an Edomite, and an Arabian mother, so not a Jew. He had been appointed "king" by the Roman senate (cf. "sceptre ... from Judah," Gen. 49:10). The "wise men" were "Magi," astrologers. Herodotus speaks of a tribe of Magi among the Medians. "East" translates a word meaning "from the risings" of the sun, so probably east of Palestine.

Matt. 2:2. "Born King" suggests a contrast. Jesus was "born King." Herod was appointed king. "Have seen" is from a verb to see with the eyes, so not an imaginary vision. "Star" is the word for one star ($ast\bar{e}r$), not a group of stars ($astron$) as some suggest. It was "his star," not "a star." Actually they saw it not *in* the eastern sky, but *while they were in the east*. "Worship" literally means to kneel or prostrate in homage or obeisance.

Matt. 2:3. "Troubled" renders a verb meaning *to agitate* as water; to trouble the mind; or, as here, to terrify.

III. DOCTRINAL VALUE.
This passage bears witness to the Kingship of Jesus Christ. It speaks of the response made to the Kingship both by inanimate nature and by human personality. *The Gospel of Matthew* emphasizes that Jesus is the King of the Jews and of the whole world.

IV. PRACTICAL AIM.
To set forth the varying responses given to the Kingship of Jesus and the resultant consequences. Regardless of a man's position he must answer the question, "What shall I do then with Jesus which is called Christ?" (Matt. 27:22).

V. HOMILETICAL FORM

Theme: "The Reception of the King."

Introduction: Even in His birth hour Jesus confronted men and nature with His claims upon them. God is sovereign in that He does that which He wills and which is in accord with His nature. But man is a person endowed with a free will. As such he is responsible for his choices. To accept God's sovereign will is to rise to the heights of greatness. To reject that will is to go down to the depths of ruin both in time and in eternity. This twofold truth is clearly demonsrated in Matthew 2.

A. *The Response of Inanimate Nature* — "His star in the east . . . ." Various efforts have been exerted to explain this phenomenon. Kepler suggested that it was a conjunction of Jupiter and Saturn in 747 A.U.C (Roman Timetable) to which was added Mars in 748. Chinese records refer to a comet in the spring of 749. Reverend C. Pritchard, as confirmed at Greenwich, suggests that the above constellation could not have appeared as one star. They were never nearer one another than double the diameter of the moon. The suggestion that the Magi had weak eyes is preposterous. The word used means *a star,* not a group of stars. A normal star would have been as far from the Magi in Bethlehem as "in the east." This star "came, and stood over where the young child was." It was a miracle. God said, "Let His star come into being," and it was so. Inanimate nature responded to God's sovereign will.

It was always true. Water, wind, vegetation, rocks, and physical disease responded to his word. "The heavens declare the glory of God; and the firmament showeth his handywork" (Ps. 19:1). The universe came into being at His word. Seasons, seed-time and harvest all respond to His will. In the realm of nature Christ is King. His law is absolute.

B. *The Response of Science* — "There came wise men. . . ." While they were astrologers they suggest the advanced wisdom of their day. They could have been Jewish proselytes who held to the Messianic hope. Even Virgil, the Roman poet, had caught such a vision.

Whatever the source of their knowledge, in faith, they followed the vision to worship and to lay their treasures at the feet of the Christ child. They followed God's guidance, refusing to make their knowledge the instrument of a tyrant bent upon defeating the purpose of God. Thus they became a symbol of science and knowledge which recognizes the source of all wisdom and dedicates it to the salvation, not the destruction, of men.

Unhappily this is not always true. Greek philosophy achieved unprecedented heights of greatness in mental power. It formed the basis of modern scientific investigation and achievement. Yet it set itself up against "the wisdom of God" (cf. I Cor. 1:20-28). Refusing to recognize God, God gave it over to a reprobate mind, one that is void of judgment (Rom. 1:28). The very wisdom of modern man has produced products which largely either corrupt man or threaten to destroy him altogether. The greatest need today is a worship of and thorough dedication to God in Christ within the realm of modern man's intellect and its fruits.

C. *The Response of Government* — "When Herod the king had heard these things, he was troubled, and all Jerusalem with him." As a non-Jew Herod had no right to the throne of Judaea. This knowledge, plus his jealous nature, led him to destroy every seeming threat to his position: his two favorite sons, Aristobulus and Alexander; his favorite wife, their mother, Mariamne; Antipater, another son; the brother and mother of Mariamne; and her uncle, his faithful adviser. Augustus Caesar said that it was better to be Herod's sow (*hus*) than his son (*huios*), for the former had a better chance to live.

Thus this suspicious and jealous king was troubled or terrified when he heard of one "that is born King of the Jews." Herod was merely *appointed* king of the Jews. He occupied the place which rightly belonged to Jesus. Wherever governments usurp the place of God they have a right to be terrified. "And all Jerusalem with him." When those in power defy God, those over whom they rule may well be terrified as well.

But Jesus had no kingly aspirations in the political sense. Had Herod joined the Magi in worship and in placing his crown at Jesus' feet, he would have received it back enhanced and glorified. For government is ordained of God for his purpose. But Herod sought to intervene between men and God's redemptive ministry. No government has that right. Soul liberty is man's right, not something bestowed or withheld by rulers.

Herod's attitude may be described in two ways. First, he feigned a desire to worship Jesus (2:7-8). Second, he desired only to destroy Jesus (2:16). His slaughter of the infants, probably about twenty, was so insignificant an event in comparison with his other murders that extra-biblical history ignores it. But God's word records it. Though secular history ignores the hypocritical lip-service paid to God and tends to minimize the destructive work of ungodly rulers, the records of God in time and eternity indelibly record them. Such nations are judged of God in the context of history. Herod died a horrible, loathsome death less than two years later. All of the Herods die, but Jesus Christ lives on in triumph over them.

D. *The Response of the Soul* — "We ... are come to worship him ... bring me word again, that I may come and worship him also" (2:2, 8). The outward attitude is the same; the inward purpose is different. The difference rested within their separate wills. The one was humble, sincere, and benevolent. The other was hypocritical, cynical, and destructive. "But the hour cometh, and now is, when the true worshippers shall worship the Father in spirit and in truth: for the Father seeketh such to worship him" (John 4:23).

True spiritual worship must be a willing response within the souls of men. Note the contrast — a babe in a manger versus the wisdom and the political power of men. But in the babe was the wisdom of God and the power of God (I Cor. 1:24). As a babe He had no power to compel either the Magi or the king. As a man He did not compel obeisance by force. It must be willingly and personally given. When this is done, men rejoice (2:10). When it is not done, men are troubled in heart, and the whole world with them (2:3).

Men withhold themselves from Him now to their own hurt and loss. But the day will come when He will be "King of Kings and Lord of Lords" (Rev. 17:14; Rev. 19:16).

Matthew 3

THE SHADOW OF COMING EVENTS

3:16. "And Jesus, when he was baptized, went up straightway out of the water: and, lo, the heavens were opened unto him, and he saw the Spirit of God descending like a dove, and lighting upon him:"

3:17. "And lo a voice from heaven, saying, This is my beloved Son, in whom I am well pleased."

I. HISTORICAL SETTING. The time is probably A.D. 26. The place is the Jordan River near Bethany. Thirty years have elapsed since Jesus' birth (Luke 3:23). This event breaks eighteen years of silence concerning Jesus (Luke 2:42). Six months earlier John the Baptist had begun his ministry as the forerunner of the Messiah. Multitudes came to hear his preaching, and many received his baptism of repentance. Word of his ministry reached Galilee. So Jesus came to present Himself for baptism. The time had arrived when the King should present himself. The Kingdom of Heaven is at hand.

II. EXPOSITORY MEANING

Matt. 3:16. "When he was baptized" translates a participle, "being baptized." "Baptize" transliterates a Greek word meaning to dip, plunge, or submerge. Metaphorically it means to be overwhelmed as by calamities. John's *baptism* (*baptismos,* not the act but its significance) was symbolically with reference to repentance, or a willingness to participate in Messiah's kingdom.

Matt. 3:16. "Spirit of God." The third person of the Trinity. This is not the Spirit's entrance into the world. He was active both in the Old Testament and in the birth of Jesus. It is an anointing of the King.

23

Matt. 3:16. "dove." It is symbolic of gentleness and sweetness. Matthew says, "As a dove." Luke says, "In a bodily shape like a dove."

Matt. 3:16. "Voice." This is the Father, the first person of the Trinity. Note the presence of the Trinity — Son, Spirit, Father.

Matt. 3:17. Literally, "This is my Son, the beloved." "Well pleased" is an aorist tense of point action covering eternity and time. It is God's approval of Jesus' life up to this point. Note also Matthew 17:5 and II Peter 1:17.

III. DOCTRINAL VALUE. In His baptism Jesus symbolized His death and resurrection, that which He did for man's redemption. This involves the triune God. Secondarily He authenticated the ministry of John; He identified Himself with man; He identified Himself with the Suffering Servant of Isaiah (cf. Isa. 40:3-5; 42:6-21; 53).

IV. PRACTICAL AIM. To reveal the King as the Suffering Servant of Jehovah in whom the triune God wrought salvation for lost men. Though a King He became one with sinful man, becoming obedient to death in the eternal Spirit. In His resurrection God declared Him to be the Son of God with power in whom the Father is well pleased. This is the heart of the Kingdom which He established.

V. HOMILETICAL FORM

Theme: "The Shadow of Coming Events."

Introduction: The author of Hebrews refers to the Levitical rituals as "a shadow of good things to come" (Heb. 10:1). In a very real sense the same may be said of Jesus' baptism. It was a shadow of coming events which would climax the redemptive purpose which God activated in the incarnation of His Son. That this purpose involved the entire Godhead is seen in this event which marked the beginning of Jesus' public ministry. Here is symbolized the truth that "God was in Christ, reconciling the world unto himself . . ." (II Cor. 5:19). This is seen in first, the baptism of the Son; second, the anointing by the Spirit; third, the approval of the Father.

A. *The Baptism of the Son* — "And Jesus, when he was

baptized . . . ." Why was Jesus baptized? Not for repentance, because He had no sin from which to repent. The sinlessness of Jesus is at the heart of the gospel. To set an example? Perhaps. To authenticate John's ministry? In a sense. As dedication for His own ministry? Possibly so. But these are fringe ideas read into the event after the fact.

What did this baptism mean to Jesus? "To be baptized" (3:13) is an infinitive of purpose. "By him" (3:13) links His ministry to that of the herald of the Kingdom, a Kingdom which is rooted in God's redemptive love whose greatest expression is seen in the crucifixion and resurrection (cf. Isa. 40:3-5; Isa. 42:21; 53). After this event Jesus spoke of His baptism only twice (Matt. 20:22; Luke 12:50) both of which referred to His death. In His initial baptism He fulfilled that which was right as He joined others who were being baptized. Sinless, yet He identified Himself with sinners as later He did on the cross. His baptism was a prophecy of His death and resurrection. Ours is a symbol of these events in which we as sinners saved by grace symbolically identify ourselves with Him who knew no sin, yet for our sake became sin, that we might become the righteousness of God through Him (Rom. 6:3-4; II Cor. 5:21).

B. *The Anointing by the Spirit* — "The Spirit of God . . . lighting upon him. . . ."

The Cerinthian Gnostics, insisting that God was neither born nor did He die, said that Deity came upon Jesus at His baptism and left Him on the cross (Matt. 27:46). But the whole of the New Testament contradicts this.

What is the significance of this anointing? It is the anointing of the King. The dove is symbolic of gentleness, innocence, and meekness (Matt. 10:16). The Levitical law prescribed one dove, along with a lamb, or two doves only for the poor, as a sacrificial offering (Lev. 12:6; Lev. 14:22; cf. Luke 2:24). This would be the primary thought suggested to Matthew's Hebrew readers.

This was not Jesus' first contact with the Holy Spirit. By Him He had been born and had developed into manhood. He will continue to be with Him. Thus this anointing was

not one of power for His ministry of mighty works and teaching. He is not to be a King in the popular Hebrew sense. It
was His anointing for sacrifice. As one who was gentle, innocent, and meek He would be the sacrifice for sin. It corresponds to the lamb and dove for those who could afford it,
or to two doves for the poor. Thus Jesus is to be the comprehensive sacrifice for sin for all who will receive Him. He will
be offered "through the eternal Spirit" (Heb. 9:14). As the
dove He is weak in His sacrifice. As the Spirit He is powerful
in His salvation.

C. *The Approval of the Father* — "This is my beloved Son
. . . well pleased."

This harks back to Psalm 2. Here the Father speaks of the
only begotten Son to whom He will give the heathen for an
inheritance. He shall be His "king upon my holy hill of
Zion." Though the heathen shall rage and kings shall plot,
the Son is promised victory. His victory shall not be military
but spiritual. The Jews looked for the former. God gives the
latter. He will go through the cross to the throne. Once again
the thought of sacrifice appears.

Note Heb. 10:5-9; Matt. 17:5; Luke 9:31; Rom. 1:4-5. The
one approved will be raised and crowned. Thus He is our
Sacrifice, Hope, and King.

Matthew 4

THE VICTORIOUS KING

4:1. "Then was Jesus led up of the Spirit into the wilderness to be tempted of the devil."

4:3. "If thou be the Son of God, command that these stones be made bread."

4:6. "If thou be the Son of God, cast thyself down . . . ."

4:9. "All these things will I give thee, if thou wilt fall down and worship me."

I. HISTORICAL SETTING. Immediately (straightway, Mark 1:12) after His baptism the Holy Spirit led (driveth, Mark 1:12) Jesus into the wilderness of Judea. The time is A.D. 26. The traditional Mount of Temptation is a wild, barren mountain just west and north of Jericho. From the time of the crusades it was called Quarantania. After forty days of fasting Jesus was tempted of the devil. The fasting was not mere ritual. It was a fasting of preoccupation with the will of God, wherein Jesus felt no hunger. "He was afterward ahungered" (Matt. 4:2). The order of the temptations varies in Matthew and Luke, with the sequence of the second and third being reversed. Luke follows the geographical order. Matthew gives the natural and climactic. At the outset of His public ministry the King faces the Adversary who challenges His right to reign.

II. EXPOSITORY MEANING

Matt. 4: "led" means to lead from a lower to a higher place, from the valley to the mountain. "Of the spirit" or by the agency of the Spirit. The choice was of God not of Satan. "To be tempted" is an infinitive of purpose meaning to test, to prove, either in the good or evil sense. God would

27

prove the good; Satan would prove the evil. Note "of the **spirit**" and "of the devil." "Devil" means slanderer. It is the proper name of a person (masculine). The Devil slanders God to man (Gen. 3:4) and man to God (Job 1:9-11).

Matt. 4:3. "If thou be [the] Son of God . . . ." A condition of the first class (Greek) assumed as true. "Command" is the imperative form of "say," a *command* of the devil for Jesus to *command*.

Matt. 4:6. "If thou be . . . ." Again a condition assumed as being true.

Matt. 4:9. "All these things" refers to the "kingdoms of the cosmos" (4:8), including the rule of the world, not merely Palestine. "Fall down and worship me" or prostrate before Satan, the usual form of oriental worship.

III. DOCTRINAL VALUE. The temptations of Jesus involve primarily both His humanity and deity. Involved also are the doctrines of Satan and of evil. The place and power of the Word of God in temptation are seen. The Messianic mission and method are evident. This entire event is cast against the background of the will of God and the way of the cross. Both the King and the nature of His Kingdom are brought into clear focus.

IV. PRACTICAL AIM. To show that in Jesus Christ we have a King or High Priest who "was in all points tempted like as we are, yet without sin" (Heb. 4:15). He is therefore able to help us when we are tempted. Here Christ truly becomes one with us; He is the Pioneer of our faith who shows the way to triumphant, Godly living.

V. HOMILETICAL FORM

Theme: "The Victorious King."

Introduction: This initial temptation of Jesus in His public ministry is the first of which there were many. Jesus, as a man, had the capacity to yield to these temptations or else they were not real. The glorious truth is that He was "tempted . . . yet without sin" (Heb. 4:15). In so doing He justified the demands of God's law. He proved Himself to be "just" or righteous in order that He might become the "justifier of him which believeth in Jesus" (Rom. 3:26). He "was in all points tempted like as we are" (Heb. 4:15). Luke says that He endured "every kind of temptation" (4:13, author's translation). Satan tempted Eve in the realms of the physical, aesthetic, and of ambition (Gen. 3:6). He tempted Jesus in the realms of physical need, spiritual trust, and divine mission. Sin is the illegitimate expression of a legitimate desire.

A. *The Realm of Physical Need* — "If thou be the Son of God, command that these stones be made bread."

Satan assumes the truth of the words of the Father at Jesus' baptism. As the Son of God Jesus should possess divine power, a power which He had not used as yet. Satan suggests that Jesus use this power for selfish ends, something that He never did. In this temptation is the subtle suggestion that God is not benevolent (cf. Gen. 3:1). Likewise he implies failure of Jesus' divine mission at the outset. Suppose that He should die of starvation. What then? Furthermore Satan suggests that Jesus assert His deity to the abandonment of His humanity or His identity with the weakness of man. Involved also is the thought that God cannot be trusted. "Take things into your own hands."

This temptation is common to every man. Man must have bread. If he cannot get it one way, then get it in another. But Jesus says, "Take no thought [be not overly anxious] for your life, what ye shall eat ... is not the life more than meat ...?" (cf. Matt. 6:25 ff.).

In essence this was Jesus' answer to Satan (Matt. 4:4). Note His use of Scripture, the sword of the Spirit, as He quoted from Deuteronomy 8:3. There is more to man than the physical body. He is a soul which feeds upon God's every word. At the very beginning the King renounces self-will for the will of God. Those who aspire to places of authority should do likewise.

B. *The Realm of Spiritual Trust* — "Cast thyself down. ..."

Once again Satan assumes the deity of Jesus. He also assumes His humanity as he appeals to the human weakness of dizziness from the heights. Basic, however, is the temptation

to doubt God's promises. To put God to such a test is to
doubt. Satan said, "Do not trust, but dare. Instead of throw-
ing yourself upon God's promise, throw yourself from the
pinnacle of the temple. Create a crisis, and call God's hand."

Note that in reply to Jesus' use of Scripture, the Devil re-
plies in kind (cf. Ps. 91:11-12). He can use Scripture to his
own nefarious ends. Note again that he misquotes by omitting
a vital part. Lifting it out of its context he seeks to create
doubt rather than faith.

The all-inclusive element of this temptation is to use the
spectacular rather than prosaic faith in God to obtain a
desired end. By such a deed Jesus would immediately receive
acclamation as the Messiah. According to God's promise it
would involve no real danger, only seem to do so. In truth it
involved hypocrisy on Jesus' part. Such acclamation would be
but surface in nature. The Kingdom could not be founded
upon such. God's purpose must be achieved in such a way
that those who received Jesus must do so in true faith. His
Kingdom must be founded upon truth, a truth which was
forged in the fires of suffering and tempered in the waters of
the resurrection. Jesus chose to be identified with a cause
which failed, according to man's standards, but which
triumphed in the will and purpose of God. Man should never
employ the risque to achieve personal or divine ends.

Thus His second reply from Scripture (Matt. 4:7; cf. Deut.
6:16). "Tempt" here is the same word as used in Matthew
4:1 with the prefixed preposition. This adds force to the
word, and clearly gives it the evil sense. He will not try God
to see if He will fail. Instead He will trust in God, knowing
that His will must succeed.

C. *The Realm of Divine Mission* — "All these things will I
give thee . . . if. . . ."

Note the rising sequence of the temptations: self-preserva-
tion; public acclamation; world domination. From "an exceeding high mountain" Jesus saw the adjoining kingdoms.
"In a moment of time" (Luke 4:5) in a vision He beheld
the "kingdoms of the cosmos," or orderly world, and their
glory. This was destined of God to be Jesus' realm. Satan

implies that such shall come to be. But note that he quotes no Scripture. Not the Father's will but only that of Jesus is to be involved. God's promise to the Son is in the background (cf. Ps. 2:8-12). The issue is not the fact but the method to be employed.

Note the false claim involved: "I will give thee . . . ." Were they his to give? Note the false method suggested: "If thou wilt fall down and worship me." Would-be conquerors have always fallen into Satan's trap and ultimately have failed. Satan promises and does not, yea, cannot deliver (cf. John 8:44-45). God promises and does deliver (cf. Matt. 5:5).

Note the two methods involved (cf. John 6:15; Matt. 27:40-43; Matt. 16:25; Luke 9:5). Note Jesus' final answer to Satan. "Begone Satan" (author's translation). cf. Deut. 6:13.

Matthew 5

THE CHARACTER OF THE CHRISTIAN

5:3. "Blessed are the poor in spirit: for theirs is the kingdom of heaven."

5:4. "Blessed are they that mourn: for they shall be comforted."

5:5. "Blessed are the meek: for they shall inherit the earth."

5:6. "Blessed are they which do hunger and thirst after righteousness: for they shall be filled."

5:7. "Blessed are the merciful: for they shall obtain mercy."

5:8. "Blessed are the pure in heart: for they shall see God."

5:9. "Blessed are the peacemakers: for they shall be called the children of God."

5:10. "Blessed are they which are persecuted for righteousness' sake: for theirs is the kingdom of heaven."

5:11. "Blessed are ye, when men shall revile you, and persecute you, and shall say all manner of evil against you falsely, for my sake."

5:12. "Rejoice, and be exceedingly glad: for great is your reward in heaven: for so persecuted they the prophets which were before you."

I. HISTORICAL SETTING. The sermon on the Mount was delivered probably near the middle of Jesus' public ministry or about A.D. 28. The place is uncertain, but it was at a level place (Luke 6:17) on a mountain (Matt. 5:1) in Galilee. It may have been the Horns of Hattin between Capernaum and Nazareth. Some scholars insist that this is not a sermon, but a collection of Jesus' sayings delivered on various occasions. Others distinguish the account of Luke from that of Matthew as being distinct sermons delivered on different occasions. But they probably are different accounts of the same sermon. After a night of prayer Jesus chose the twelve apostles (Mark 3:13-19; Luke 6:12-16). The sermon was delivered to the Twelve although the "multitude" heard it also. In it Jesus set forth the character and conditions of life pertaining to citizens of His Kingdom. It has been called the Constitution of the Kingdom of God. Doctor Oswald Dykes called it "The Manifesto of the King."

II. EXPOSITORY MEANING

Matt. 5:3. "Blessed" means "happy," not a gift from without but a condition of character realized within one's life, and resulting in happiness or blessedness. "Poor" means deep poverty (cf. Luke 16:20, 22). "In spirit" is a recognition of spiritual poverty as the publican (Luke 18:13).

Matt. 5:4. "mourn." This means to be sad, to lament, not only over one's own sins, but over the sins of others. The "poor in spirit" will "mourn." "Comforted" is the verb from which comes "Comforter' (John 14:16), the one called alongside for comfort or encouragement.

Matt. 5:5. "meek." This is not effeminacy but the inner calm of strength. The meek man recognizes the source of this strength and seeks to use it for God's glory and man's blessedness.

Matt. 5:6. "hunger" and "thirst." These are the primary drives, food and drink. "Righteousness" is personal righteousness, but which is desired for all men. Jesus gives to these natural drives a spiritual content. "Filled" is used of feeding and fattening cattle.

Matt. 5:7. "merciful." This quality means full of mercy, pity, or compassion as opposed to censorious criticism (cf. Matt. 7:1-2). This is the law of sowing and reaping.

Matt. 5:8. "pure in heart." This purity is not outer but inner cleanliness. The Jews practiced the opposite.

Matt. 5:9. "peacemakers." Over against warmongers Jesus acclaims the makers of peace. The primary reference is with respect to peace between God and man. The Son of God is the perfect peacemaker (cf. Eph. 2:14 f.). Such shall be like Him.

Matt. 5:10. "persecuted." This word sometimes means to pursue in a good sense. Here it means to pursue with malignity.

Matt. 5:11. "revile." This means to "reproach" (ASV) or to insult with evil language. "Falsely" is a participle meaning "lying."

Matt. 5:12. "Rejoice . . . exceeding glad." The first word is the common word for joy. The latter words denote exhultation in joy (cf. Luke 6:23, "leap" for joy).

III. DOCTRINAL VALUE. The Beatitudes set forth the character of the Kingdom man. This character involves the nature of the Kingdom as an inner condition resulting in outward attitudes and aptitudes. Involved is the contrast between the Messianic kingdom envisioned by the Jews and the Kingdom as seen through the eyes of Jesus.

IV. PRACTICAL AIM. To see the Christian character not as something to possess but as a *being* and *doing* for Christ's sake. The Christian life is a gift of grace. But it is more than a gift. It is a stewardship of character to be developed and used in bringing the rule of God into the hearts of all men.

V. HOMILETICAL FORM
Theme: "The Character of the Christian"

Introduction: When the King would set forth the nature of His Kingdom, He turned His back upon a popular movement and selected a small group of men. The nature of the Kingdom which He declared to them was in direct contrast to that sought by the masses. During the four hundred years between Malachi and Matthew Jewish literature created the popular image of a conquering military Messiah whose reign would be characterized by power, pomp, and plenty. In sharp contrast Jesus pictures His reign as one of submission, service, and suffering. As such the King's followers are not to be soldiers but "salt" (5:13), not legions but "light" (5:14). It is not a matter of conquest but of character. This character is presented as essence, expression, and experience.

A. *The Essence of Christian Character* — "Blessed ... poor in spirit ... mourn ... meek ... hunger and thirst ... ."

Happiness (blessedness) is the desired goal of every man. False roads lead to frustration. Those who first heard these words of Jesus, including the Twelve, followed the path of performance and possessing. Jesus emphasized the importance of being and sharing. After two thousand years man follows the former and ignores the latter. The enigma of man is the paradox of Jesus. Natural man says, "Happy . . . the rich . . . joyful . . . proud . . . satisfied." Jesus says, "Happy . . . the poor . . . mournful . . . meek . . . hungry." Note the progression in Matthew 5:3-6.

The "poor in spirit" is conscious of his spiritual need, and thus surrenders to the will of the King (5:3). Aware of his own inability, he is willing to be governed. Such receives the Kingdom as he submits to the King. Recognizing his weakness he *mourns* for his own sins and those of others (5:4). But he is comforted by Him who stands alongside him in forgiveness and strength. Thus he realizes the inner strength of *meekness* (5:5). He achieves happiness not in new circumstances, but his happiness alters his circumstances. Thus he inherits the earth. Therefore he *hungers and thirsts* more and more for a richer experience with the King, not for himself alone but for all men (5:6). In his submission he receives a continuous infilling of the Spirit, who enables him to experience *happiness* and to share it with others who through his zeal are brought to submit to the King.

B. *The Expression of Christian Character* — "Blessed . . . the merciful ... pure in heart ... peacemakers ... ."

Note again the progression in Matthew 5:7-9. The passive essence of Christian character evolves into the active expression of that character in evangelistic zeal. Such a person does not give way to captious criticism of those who lack the Christian character. Rather he is "merciful" (5:7) as he declares God's love and grace to them. In so doing he receives not their judgment (Matt. 7-12), but their mercy in return. It is "a self-acting law of the moral world" (Bruce). In such an attitude the Christian becomes "pure in heart" (5:8). His heart is undivided as he presses his one aim in life — to share Christian happiness with others. With absolute loyalty to the King, he sees God in the fulness of His love and grace, for himself and for all men. So wherever he goes he exemplifies the atmosphere of peace (5:9). Not only is he at peace within himself and with God, but he is a *peacemaker* between man and man and between God and man. As such he becomes like the King (Eph. 2:14-16), and in truth is a child of God.

C. *The Experience of Christian Character* — "Persecuted ...revile...."

Verses 10-12 retrogress to verses 3-9. Jesus never promised the Christian "flow'ry beds of ease" (cf. Matt. 16:24; John 16:33). But He does promise happiness in tribulation. The Christian is not to seek suffering for suffering's sake. It is to be found only in his zeal after righteousness (5:10) as He does the will of the King (5:11). The Christian character should never *deserve* persecution and reproach. Neither should he seek to avoid it in the line of duty. In his suffering he is in a glorious succession (the prophets) and a royal one (the King Himself); cf. Heb. 2:10.

Matthew 6

THE PRIMACY OF KINGDOM VALUES

6:1. "Take heed that ye do not your alms before men, to be seen of them . . . ."

6:2. "Therefore when thou doest thine alms, do not sound a trumpet before thee, as the hypocrites do in the synagogues and in the streets, that they may have glory of men. Verily I say unto you, They have their reward."

6:5. "And when thou prayest . . . ."

6:16. "Moreover when ye fast . . . ."

6:19. "Lay not up for yourselves treasures upon earth . . . ."

6:33. "But seek ye first the kingdom of God, and his righteousness; and all these things shall be added unto you."

I. HISTORICAL SETTING. This is a continuance of the Sermon on the Mount. The King turns from essential character and social relationship to the personal righteousness of the Kingdom man as it relates him to God and His rule. It is a contrast of current practices in religion with the pure motives which should activate the Kingdom man with respect to the kingdom of this world and to the Kingdom of God.

II. EXPOSITORY MEANING

Matt. 6:1. "Take heed." This is an imperative form meaning to set the mind. Followed by the negative particle *(mē)*, as here, it means to beware. G. Campbell Morgan calls it the "flaming sword" guarding holy ground. "Alms" translates the word for "righteousness." It includes alms (6:2), prayer (6:5), and fasting (6:16). "To be seen" is an infinitive of purpose. From it comes our word *theatrical.*

Matt. 6:2. "alms." The word means any eleemosynary deed. It does not refer to church finances. "Trumpet." Preceded by

39

the negative particle it means "stop sounding a trumpet." Jewish writings do not list such a practice. But it probably refers to the custom of some to sound a small trumpet to call beggars to them and to advertise their generosity. "Hypocrites." This is a theatrical word (cf. 6:1) for *play actor,* one who plays a part. Only Jesus applied this word to men (cf. Matt. 23). "They have their reward." "They have" renders an intensive form of *have.* The papyri lists it as a commercial term meaning "payment in full."

Matt. 6:16. "fast." This is self-denial in communion with God. It could be good (Matt. 4:2) or evil, as here. The motive flavors the act.

Matt. 6:19. "Lay not up." This is an imperative preceded by the negative. Literally, "stop laying up." "Treasures." The word means *caskets* (Matt. 2:11) or *storehouses* (Matt. 13.52). Here it means that which is stored up. In this instance it could include "reward" as contrasted in Matthew 6:1-2, 5, 16, as well as material goods. "Yourselves." Literally this means "to you" rather than to God.

Matt. 6:33. "seek." This is an imperative form meaning to desire, to strive to obtain that which is desired. "First the kingdom and the righteousness of him." "God" is not in the best manuscripts. "First" is in the emphatic position. The definite article before *kingdom* and *righteousness* emphasizes both. "And all these things shall be added unto you." "These things" refer primarily to physical benefits, but include "reward" also. "Added." This means here "to super-add," abundance.

III. DOCTRINAL VALUE. This chapter bears witness to true Kingdom values as over against worldly aims and desires. The former is inner and spiritual rather than outer and material. Such values are indestructible. The Kingdom man seeks a proper relationship with God rather than the plaudits of men. Involved is the true righteousness versus the ostentatious hypocrisy of those outside the Kingdom. This includes a proper concept of charity, prayer, and fasting. The true treasures are those of the heart. Singlehearted devotion to God supersedes every other possession. The whole passage teaches the primacy of God's rule and righteousness.

IV. PRACTICAL AIM. To enable the Christian to seek to be well pleasing to God as he places the values of life in their relative importance. By way of suggestion it is to challenge lost men to seek first God's will and way in the renunciation of that which perishes and fades away.

V. HOMILETICAL FORM

Theme: "The Primacy of Kingdom Values."

Introduction: The Christian is a citizen of two worlds, the earthly and the heavenly, with each striving for the mastery (cf. Rom. 7:14-25). As such the Kingdom man becomes a battleground between God and man, and God and mammon. In this conflict the good becomes the enemy of the best. In Chapter 5 Jesus warns His followers against the evils which assail them in their relationships to other men. Now He warns against the subtler temptations in their relationship to God. If Satan cannot defile them through personal or social sins, he will attack them in the realm of personal righteousness, that which would rightly relate their lives to the will of God. The Christian can do *right* things in the *wrong* way. The result is sin. Jesus warns against such as He pictures the lure of man, the love of mammon, and the loyalty to God.

A. *The Lure of Man* — "To be seen of them . . . ."

Because of his new nature the Kingdom man is inclined toward deeds of righteousness. Satan, knowing that he can not stifle this desire, seeks to pervert it to evil ends. He directs it toward men rather than toward God. "To be seen" is an infinitive of purpose. Thusly perverted man's purpose is to receive the praise of men rather than to receive divine commendation and benefits. This truth Jesus illustrates with three righteous deeds: alms, prayer, and fasting.

The logical order reverses that which Jesus used. True "fasting" is self-denial resulting from a pre-occupation with the will of God. "Prayer" is communion between God and man. "Alms" is but the outward expression of the God-likeness of the Kingdom man whose giving stems from the grace of God. Fasting evolves into prayer which results in the spirit of giving. When directed toward God alone, they become true righteousness. But "before men" they are perverted into selfish, hypocritical deeds for self-glory.

Note the outcome of such righteousness. It is not that they may appear unto God to fast, but "unto men" (6:16). It is to be "seen of men," not heard of God, that they pray (6:5). The end of their charity is "that they may have glory of men" (6:2). This is in contrast with the Kingdom ideal (5:16).

Men receive that for which they seek. "They have their reward." They seek to be seen of and glorified by men. They receive it. *Paid in full!* To such God has no obligation.

B. *The Love of Mammon.* "For yourselves treasures upon earth . . . ."

The Bible does not discourage the making of money. It exhorts to diligence in business, thrift, and the stewardship of wealth. But Satan perverts these virtues into miserliness. Against such the Kingdom man is warned.

The rich fool is not accused of dishonesty. His sin lay in the wrong purpose in the hoarding of wealth. Of him Jesus said, "These things are requiring thy soul [life] of thee" (Luke 12:20, author's translation). Note Jesus' words about inordinate anxiety (Matt. 6:25 ff.).

"For where your treasure is, there will your heart be also" (6:21). Likewise, "where your heart is, there will your treasure be also."

The Kingdom man must make money honestly, invest money wisely, and dedicate money religiously. He cannot serve two masters (6:24).

C. *The Loyalty to God.* "Seek ye first . . . ."

Note the order of "first" things: "the kingdom of him;" "the righteousness of him." His Kingdom, the rule of God, is primary over the rule of man. A man must first submit to the rule of God in his own life. Then the coming of the Kingdom in other men's lives must be the Kingdom man's first desire. The first real petition of the Model Prayer (6:10) is "Thy kingdom come . . . ." Before daily bread (6:11) comes the Kingdom. God must supersede mammon in his loyalty.

"The righteousness of him" must displace self-righteousness

in the Kingdom man. Money, fasting, prayer, and alms to him are not the means to an end — self-glory, self-righteousness — but the outgrowth of God's righteousness which indwells him. Only thus may they fulfil their purpose in the will of God.

When a man is rightly related to God "all these things" shall be "super-added" to him.

Matthew 7

THE GOLDEN RULE

7:12 "*Therefore all things whatsoever ye would that men should do unto you, do ye even so to them: for this is the law and the prophets.*"

I. HISTORICAL SETTING. The Golden Rule comes near the close of the Sermon on the Mount. Luke (6:31) places it just after Matthew 5:42. This verse complements Matthew 5:17. These two verses may well be regarded as parentheses which encompass all that comes between. In its immediate setting the Golden Rule is a climax to Matthew 7:1-12. The Kingdom man is warned against condemnatory judgment (7:1-5), but is called upon to exercise discrimination (7:6). To exercise properly these elements he is to ask, seek, and knock in order to be empowered of God. It is in such power that he is able to exercise the Golden Rule.

II. EXPOSITORY MEANING

Matt. 7:12. "Therefore." This word harks back not only to Matthew 5:17 ff. It calls for reexamination of Matthew 7:1-11 in particular. It calls for soul-searching.

Matt. 7:12. "All things." This is one word in Greek, and precedes "therefore." It is thus in the emphatic position. "Therefore" is followed by "whatsoever." "All things . . . whatsoever" emphasize the scope of that which Jesus has in mind.

Matt. 7:12. "would." This translates a verb "to will." It is more than a mere wish, but delves into man's will.

Matt. 7:12. "should do." This is a subjunctive form, "all things . . . whatsoever . . . men should do . . . ." The scope of possibilities is infinite.

Matt. 7:12. Literally, "so also you do [imperative] to them." "You" is emphatic.

III. DOCTRINAL VALUE. In this verse Jesus laid down the comprehensive rule for Christian conduct with regard to all men. It does not, except by implication, touch upon one's responsibility to God. This is not a justification for a purely social gospel. It furnishes a guide for the Kingdom man in all of his social relationships. The Christian religion is both Godward and manward (cf. Matt. 22:37-40). Only as one is rightly related in the former may he achieve the latter.

IV. PRACTICAL AIM. To show that the Kingdom man is not to be burdened with a multiplicity of rules of conduct. There is but one rule: love for God and man. The latter will never exceed the former; and without the former the latter is impossible.

V. HOMILETICAL FORM
   Theme: "The Golden Rule."

Introduction: God simplifies; man complicates. This is true whether one considers the plan of salvation or the personal living of the saved man. The question is constantly being asked, "Is it right to do this or that?" Volumes have been written in an effort to answer this question in the realms of diplomacy, ethics, philosophy, psychology, sociology, and religion. Jesus answers it with one simple statement — the Golden Rule. It is unique, inclusive, and conclusive.

A. *It is Unique* — "Whatsoever ye would that men should do to you, do ye ... to them ...."

Some insist that this is not a new teaching, but an old one in new dress. As proof, various teachers are cited. Confucius: "Do not unto others that which you would not they should do unto you." Socrates: "What stirs your anger when done to you by others, that do not to others." Philo: "One must not himself do what he hates to have done to him." Hillel: "What is hateful to thee, do not do to another. This is the whole law; the rest is explanation of it."

But there is a decided difference. These rules are negative; that of Jesus is positive. These are passive; that is active. Theirs is the "Silver Rule;" Jesus' is the "Golden Rule." The "silver" is prohibitory; the "golden is exhortatory. The Silver

Rule prohibits murder, theft, falsehood, and adultery. The Golden Rule commands love, giving, truth, and purity. The former forbids the criminal act; the latter exhorts to Christian living. One can abide by the Silver Rule even though he passively watches another starve, so long as he does not kill him. The Golden Rule demands that one feed another to preserve his life. The one is the basis of human ethics; the other is the basis of Christian morality.

Lesser teachers taught but gave no power with which to obey. Jesus taught and empowered His followers for obedience (Matt. 7:7 ff.). Out of self respect the worldly man may do the former. But only by divine power may the Kingdom man continuously do the latter.

B. *It is Inclusive* — "Therefore all things whatsoever . . . men . . . to them . . . ."

Certain situations have been cited thus far in the Sermon. But Jesus does not stop there. The Christian cannot cite chapter and verse for every situation. Jesus did not teach rote rules for specific situations. He laid down a principle to cover all experiences. "Therefore" recaps the specifics of Matthew 5:17--7:11. "All things whatsoever" includes the general, covering the whole of life. "Man . . . to them" is not limited to blood kin, friends, neighbors, or Christians. It involves strangers, enemies, foreigners, all racial and national groups, unbelievers, — not all men *en masse,* but every man as an individual.

In short Jesus said, "Put yourself in another's place. Then act accordingly." If this simple rule were followed what wars, crimes, and injustices would be prevented! What peace, social benefits, and righteousness would result! Living by the Silver Rule has turned the world into a sea of misery, suspicion, and conflict. Redeemed men living by the Golden Rule would bring the Kingdom of God into the hearts of men.

C. *It is Conclusive* — "For this is the law and the prophets."

This is the King's answer to those who said that He would disannul the law and the prophets. Instead He endues each Kingdom man with a power which brings the law and the prophets to their intended end. The Law said, "Thou shalt have no other gods before me" (Exod. 20:3). It said, "Thou shalt love the Lord thy God with all thy heart . . . soul . . . mind" (Deut. 6:5). Only the Kingdom man can do this. The Law said, "Thou shalt not kill . . . commit adultery . . . steal . . . bear false witness against thy neighbor" (Exod. 20:13-16). It said, ". . . thou shalt love thy neighbor as thyself" (Lev. 19:18). Only the Kingdom man can do this.

Since the Golden Rule stems from the law and the prophets, it follows that only the Kingdom man possesses the qualities intended by Jesus. Wrong motives produce the wrong results. In the hands of a criminal, this rule would produce crime. Only when it is followed by a Kingdom man may its fruits be the God-kind-of-righteousness.

In Jesus, not only the law but the prophets as well, find their fulfilment. He not only taught the Golden Rule, but He followed it. His life certifies this. Its supreme example is in His death. On the cross every vestige of Isaiah found its complete fulfilment (cf. also Ps. 22). Jesus put Himself in man's place.

". . . Christ also suffered for us, leaving us an example, that ye should follow his steps: who did no sin, neither was guile found in his mouth: who, when he was reviled, reviled not again; when he suffered, he threatened not: but committed himself to him that judgeth righteously: Who his own self bare our sins in his own body on the tree, that we, being dead to sins, should live unto righteousness: by whose stripes ye were healed" (I Peter 2:21-24).

Matthew 8

A STUDY IN CONTRASTS

8:24. "And, behold, there arose a great tempest in the sea . . . but he was asleep."

8:25. And his disciples came to him, and awoke him, saying, Lord, save us: we perish."

8:26. "And he saith unto them, Why are ye fearful, O ye of little faith? Then he arose, and rebuked the winds and the sea; and there was a great calm."

8:27. "But the men marveled, saying, What manner of man is this, that even the winds and the sea obey him!"

I. HISTORICAL SETTING. This event followed shortly the Sermon on the Mount. According to A. T. Robertson's *A Harmony of the Gospels* it marks the end of Jesus' "Busy Day." Fitting Matthew's Gospel into the framework of Mark's Gospel, Doctor Robertson places it in the early evening of a day marked by many striking events (Mark 3:19 — 4:34; Matt. 12:22 — 13:53; Luke 8:4-21). This may be confusing to some. But Synoptic Criticism has proved the probable priority of Mark. It shows that Matthew and Luke, for the most part, followed the framework of Mark, while using other sources as well. The event occurred while Jesus and the Twelve were crossing the Sea of Galilee from west to east. Sudden windstorms rushing down the canyons focussing on this sea are common even today.

II. EXPOSITORY MEANING
Matt. 8:24. "tempest." The Greek word is *seismos,* like seismograph, or earthquake. The sea was turbulent as an earthquake. Mark and Luke call it a whirlwind. "asleep." The Greek tense (imperfect) means "He kept on sleeping."

49

Matt. 8:25. "Lord." This word may mean "sir" or "lord," as one over others. Here it means deity, probably in the sense of "Lord" in the Old Testament, the usual translation in the KJV for Jehovah.

"Save . . . perish." "Save" (aorist) means rescue from danger, heal from disease, or spiritual salvation. The first meaning applies here. "Save at once" "Perish" means to destroy utterly. The present passive voice as here means "we are being utterly destroyed."

Matt. 8:26. "O ye of little faith." In Greek this is one word meaning one whose faith is small and weak. "Was a great calm." "Was" is an aorist tense. "Immediately there was a great calm," a miracle. Note the contrast: "a great tempest" (8:24) ; "a great calm" (8:26) .

Matt. 8:27. "marveled." This is an ingressive aorist of the verb to wonder with admiration and/or astonishment. They "began to marvel."

Matt. 8:27. "What manner of man . . . !" This is one word in Greek. Basically, "of what country!" Here it may mean "what kind " or "how great!"

Matt. 8:27. "obey." It translates a compound verb meaning "to hear under" with the idea of submission or obedience. The present tense suggests continuous action.

III. DOCTRINAL VALUE. This passage teaches the King's miraculous power. Indeed this is the thought throughout Chapter 8. The physical (disease), natural (wind and sea), and spiritual (demons) elements obeyed His will. The will of man refused Him. This chapter sets forth the sovereignity of God and the free will of man (8:34) .

IV. PRACTICAL AIM. To contrast the faith of man and the faith of the King; the power of God's will and of man's will. The physical and natural realms are submissive to God's will. The will of man rebels to its own loss.

V. HOMILETICAL FORM
   Theme: "A Study in Contrasts."
Introduction: This is a chapter marked by great contrasts: the plight of the leper and the power of Jesus (8:2-4) ; the

faith of a pagan and the doubt of Israel (8:5-13) ; the fever
of a woman and the fortitude of the Son of Man (8:14-15) ;
the great tempest and the great calm (8:23-27) ; the grace of
God toward a demoniac and the greed of men toward their
swine (8:28-34) . It is a contrast between the power of evil
and the power of God. Note the varied expressions of evil:
disease, storm, demons, and greed; and the varied methods of
divine power: touch of the hand and the spoken word. The
focal point of contrast is seen in verses 24-27. Here we see
fear versus faith, futility versus fortitude, and astonishment
versus achievement.

A. *Fear versus Faith* — "Why are ye fearful?" (8:26) . "But
he was asleep" (8:24) .

The sea rocked and rolled as if in the teeth of an earthquake. The frail boat was enveloped in the waves. The
turmoil in nature was transferred to the spirits of the Twelve.
They feared for their boat and for their lives. But a deeper
fear seized them, fear for the safety of Jesus. What if He
should perish? What would happen to His mission and Kingdom? In all this natural and spiritual turmoil Jesus "was
asleep." No fear raged within Him.

To their cry Jesus replied, "Why are ye fearful, O ye of
little faith?" Their fear was the product of their lack of
faith: faith in Jesus' ability to care for them; faith in the
providence and purpose of God. So long as they were with
Jesus they were safe. So long as the King was in the boat
it could not sink. Any cause centered in Jesus will succeed.

Fear is always due to the absence of faith. So long as we
are in the will of God there is no place for fear. Though
the forces of evil may seem to be on the verge of triumph,
God is still in control. The sleep of Jesus was not one of
unconcern but one of confidence. So long as He is in such
a sleep, we have nothing to fear. The ship of God's purpose
is plowing through the waves of adversity toward the haven
of God's will and peace.

B. *Futility versus Fortitude* — "Lord, save us: we perish."

This boat was manned by skilful seamen. Jesus was a land-
lubber. The Twelve, through their own skill, had weathered

many storms. Now they had done their best. But still the ship threatened to sink. They had come to their wits end. Futility characterized their every effort. It was then that they turned to the Lord.

This is the essence of true prayer. Men do not really pray until they come to the end of their own abilities. Prayer is too often an escape hatch from the seat of responsibility. So long as man can do, he should. When he has reached the end of his own powers, he should *awaken* the Lord (8:25). "Man's extremity is God's opportunity."

What these men of the sea could not do, the God of the sea did. Their power was finite; His infinite. His strength is made perfect in our weakness.

C. *Astonishment versus Achievement* — "What manner of man is this, that even the wind and the sea obey him."

Apparently the previous miracles recorded in this chapter did not overly impress the Twelve. But the spectacular nature of the miracle at sea aroused astonishment and admiration. Literally, "The men began to marvel . . . the sea kept on obeying him." While man wonders, God keeps on working. Men marvel at the healing *miracles* of medical science, but the healing power is of God. Men are astonished at the space miracles of science, but the laws are the laws of God.

But the greatest miracle was yet to come. cf. Mark 5:15; Luke 15:7.

Matthew 9

THE PHYSICIAN OF SOULS

9:11. "And when the Pharisees saw it, they said unto his disciples, Why eateth your master with publicans and sinners?"

9:12. "But when Jesus heard that, he said unto them, They that be whole need not a physician, but they that are sick."

9:13. "...for I am not come to call the righteous, but sinners to repentance."

I. HISTORICAL SETTING. According to A. T. Robertson's *A Harmony of the Gospels* this event is placed in the great Galilean ministry prior to the Sermon on the Mount. Jesus had just called Matthew from his business as a tax-gatherer to follow Him as His disciple, later to become an apostle. In recognition of the occasion Matthew gave a dinner in Jesus' honor. To it were invited Jesus' disciples, and other publicans, perhaps friends and fellow tax-gatherers with Matthew. Others, called "sinners," also were guests. In keeping with the custom of the time others, including the Pharisees and some of John the Baptist's disciples, stood about and watched as the guests ate. Eating with publicans and sinners Jesus violated the customs of the Pharisees. In answer to their criticism Jesus taught a great spiritual truth.

II. EXPOSITORY MEANING

Matt. 9:11. "Pharisees." They were the conservative religious party of Jesus' day. They accepted all of the Old Testament as Scripture, believing in angels, miracles, and the resurrection from the dead. In contrast with the Sadducees, rationalists and more political than religious, who accepted only the Mosaic writings and denied angels, miracles, and the resurrection, the Pharisees were more numerous but less politically powerful. In interpreting their Scriptures the Pharisees had devised a multitude of customs and rules which were burdensome to obey.

Matt. 9:11. "master." This means "teacher," in contrast with their teachers who refrained from social contacts with publicans and sinners. While in some versions "Master" is capitalized, they did not so use the word.

Matt. 9:11. "publicans and sinners. " "Publican" renders a word meaning one who collects public revenue. The English word is from the Latin *publicanus,* one who did public duty. Roman taxes were farmed out to the highest bidder, who, in turn, employed others to collect the taxes. They were noted for graft and extortion, and were considered as traitors to their nation. As such they were commonly regarded as the companions of sinners, hence "publicans and sinners," social outcasts.

Matt. 9:12. "whole." This means in good health. "Physician" is one who heals. The sense here is physical healing, but it implies the spiritual element also. "Sick." This renders an adverb, "ill, badly." Its root carries the basic thought of evil. Both the physical and spiritual aspects are involved here. This was probably a common proverb.

Matt. 9:13. "righteous, but sinners." This transfers the thought from a social to a spiritual connotation. "To repentance," while implied, is not in the best manuscripts.

III. DOCTRINAL VALUE. This passage presents the King as a social being whose compassion reaches out to all men, regardless of their social strata. It involves a recognition of the true nature of sin. Here the Saviour is seen as the friend of sinners, the Physician of souls.

IV. PRACTICAL AIM. To point out that all men, regardless of social position or culture, are sinners in need of a Saviour. Men judge by outward appearances and conduct. Jesus looks to inner attitudes and needs. The greater sin involves the latter not the former.

V. HOMILETICAL FORM
    Theme: "The Physician of Souls"

Introduction: Jesus was a social being. But His social activities were purposeful. As a physician must come into contact with the diseased bodies of men, so the Great Physician was bound to experience intimate contact with social outcasts. He dealt with their sin, but Himself was free from it. Herein is the example for those who would follow Him. Many lessons are taught by this passage, but three are outstanding: the wrong diagnosis; the logical deduction; the proper treatment.

A. *The Wrong Diagnosis* — "publicans and sinners."

The Pharisees, then and now, assume that sin is only outward. To be sure "out of the abundance of the heart the mouth speaketh" (Matt. 12:34). But the outward expression is but the revelation of an inward condition. The mortal disease is not always evident to the natural, untrained eye. The Pharisees were quack practitioners posing as specialists.

The Great Physician rightly diagnoses all diseases. He recognized the illness in the souls of the publicans and sinners. But He also saw the more vicious disease in the hearts of the Pharisees (cf. Heb. 4:12-13). Note Jesus' reference to Micah 6:6-8 (Matt. 9:13). Outwardly the Pharisees were healthy. Inwardly their souls were sick unto death as seen in their unmerciful, critical attitude, with regard both to God and to man.

Jesus never condoned outward sin. But His most serious condemnation was directed toward wrong spiritual attitudes, especially hypocrisy (Matt. 23). Man is careful about the outward and careless about the inward disease, physical and spiritual. God is concerned about both.

B. *The Logical Deduction* — "whole need not a physician, but they that are sick."

This is a logical conclusion. Since the Pharisees regard the publicans and sinners as ill, where else would they expect the Physician to be? But there is also irony in Jesus' words. Who are the real victims of disease? With one reference to the Scriptures which the Pharisees claimed to know so well, Jesus wipes the cosmetics of self-righteousness from their pallid faces, and flashes before them the "X-ray" of their own souls. Therefore, they also need to see the Physician. The ministry of the gospel is necessary both in the slums and in the choice residential districts, in palaces as well as in hovels, to the up-and-outs as well as to the down-and-outs. "Rescue missions" are just as necessary on Park Avenue as in the Bowery. "For all have sinned, and come short of the glory of God" (Rom. 3:23).

C. *The Proper Treatment* — ". . . I am not come to call the righteous, but sinners to repentance."

In the original Greek "not" is emphatic. It emphasizes in a negative way the positive purpose of Jesus. He does not call the Pharisees "righteous," but ironically takes them at their word. In His sight they are the greater sinners, but more hopelessly so, because they are unaware of their condition.

Hardly will a man seek a physician unless he believes himself to be ill. The greater his recognition of his illness, the more anxious he is to see the physician. Hence the "publicans and sinners." However great the disease or its inroads, no man should consider himself incurable. By his own skill he may be, but the skill of the physician is another matter (cf. Ps. 103:3).

So Jesus calls all sinners, excluding none. He calls you. But the Physician cannot heal you unless you submit yourself to Him.

Matthew 10

THE DEMANDS OF DISCIPLESHIP

10:32. "Whosoever therefore shall confess me before men, him will I confess also before my Father which is in heaven."

10:33. "But whosoever shall deny me before men, him will I also deny before my Father which is in heaven."

10:34. "Think not that I am come to send peace on earth: I came not to send peace, but a sword."

10:39. "He that findeth his life shall lose it: and he that loseth his life for my sake shall find it."

I. HISTORICAL SETTING. Following A. T. Robertson's *A Harmony of the Gospels,* this chapter comes sometime after the Sermon on the Mount. Since then Jesus has taught and trained the twelve apostles. Now he sends them forth on their first independent evangelistic mission through Galilee. He told them where to go, reminded them of their message, what equipment to carry, the dangers awaiting them, and how they were to meet them. But they will receive no worse treatment than their Master already has endured. But they are not to be afraid. The heavenly Father who watches over the sparrows most assuredly will care for them. He closed this first *commission* by stating the conditions of discipleship. He will not judge the Twelve by statistical results but by their faithfulness to duty.

II. EXPOSITORY MEANING

Matt. 19:32. "whosoever." Actually this translates two words, literally, "all whosoever." It emphasizes the inclusion of all without exception. "Confess." Twice it is a future tense involving all future time. This is a changeless condition. "Confess" in Matthew 10:32 is literally "confess in me"

57

and "confess in him." In both cases "in" means "in the sphere of." Note the intimate relationship between Christ and the one confessing. "Before" here and in verse 33 means in front of, or before the face of.

Matt. 10:33. "Deny." In Matthew 10:33a it is an aorist tense suggesting complete and final denial of Christ. "Before men" suggests a public denial. This will result in Jesus' denial of such before God. Jesus impresses the Twelve with the gravity of their mission.

Matt. 10:34. "Think not." It is an aorist subjunctive preceded by a negative particle. Possibly the Twelve were thinking only of peace. Jesus said, "Stop thinking" thusly. "Send." This word, meaning to cast or throw, twice appears as an aorist infinitive of instant action. Just as the Twelve expected Jesus to send immediate peace, He hurled a sword into their midst.

Matt. 10:39. "Findeth . . . loseth" are aorist participles of definite, point action. They refer to definite, final decisions as to one's attitude. Note the paradox: "findeth . . . shall lose . . . loseth . . . shall find." The word "life" in both instances is the same, meaning either physical or spiritual life. Here it means first one and then the other. The paradox turns upon these meanings.

III. DOCTRINAL VALUE. In these verses Jesus sets forth the conditions inherent in being a Christian. Herein are found the basis of Kingdom citizenship, the absolute Lordship of the King, and the path to triumphant Kingdom living. The King makes strong demands, but He gives great rewards.

IV. PRACTICAL AIM. To show that Jesus never tried to make His way attractive. He sought only those who were willing to pay the price. To both Jesus and man Satan offers the easy path. Jesus rejected it, and so must those who would follow Him. The road to the throne leads through the cross.

V. HOMILETICAL FORM
   Theme: "The Demands of Discipleship."
Introduction: One of the greatest problems in present-day churches is the inactive member. Once enthusiastic, they have

grown cold and indifferent. Trials and the desire for easy living take their toll. Certainly one explanation of this is the manner in which members are received. Lenient standards may pad the church rolls, but they do not produce genuine, faithful followers of Christ. Jesus never sought numbers for numbers' sake. He emphasized not quantity but quality. This is seen in His instructions given to the Twelve as they launched forth on their first evangelistic effort as a group. The demands of discipleship are listed as confession, conflict, and consecration.

A. *The Demand for Confession* — "... confess me before, men, him will I also confess ...."

To confess is to declare a thing to be true and to commit one's self to it. A Christian confession is an open declaration of the truth of the gospel in Christ, and a commitment to Him. Note the confession "before men." It is more than a verbal statement. It is to choose a way of life and to walk in it. To confess "in Christ" is to place one's self in the whole sphere of Christ. Paul's phrase "in Christ" in another way of saying it.

Note that of such a person Jesus says that before the Father He will "confess in him." The man in Christ and Christ in the man presents him blameless before God (cf. John 15:1-8). Before man the Christian says of Christ, "He is mine." Before God Christ says of the Christian, "He is mine." In like fashion the man who ultimately, publicly, and finally says of Christ, "I know Him not," of him before the Father Christ says, "I know him not." Note that in both confession and denial, God holds man responsible. Christ's work for man's redemption is finished. God now calls upon man to act.

B. *The Demand for Conflict* — "... not to send peace, but a sword."

Too often the evangelist and the evangelized look beyond confession to immediate peace. It is not so with Jesus. He demands absolute loyalty which often produces conflict. The gospel unites to Christ, but it may divide from men. Even the intimate family circle may be broken. In early Christian

persecution, the informants often were members of one's own
household (10:36).

The true Christian must be prepared to pay a price for
his faith. The word "loveth" in Matthew 10:37 has to do
with choice, not with mere emotion (cf. Rom. 9:13). He
must be ready even to die, if necessary for his faith in Christ
(10:38). To take up one's cross meant to bear it to the
place of crucifixion. In Paul's day to confess "Jesus is Lord"
(Rom. 10:9, author's translation) rather than "Caesar is
Lord," could mean death. "Faithful unto death" means
"faithful unto the point of dying" (Rev. 2:10). Jesus does
not ask His disciples to do more than He did, but He asks
no less.

C. *The Demand of Consecration* — "... findeth his life ...
loseth his life for my sake shall find it."

The Christian life is a paradox. Jesus lives by dying. So
do His disciples. Satan offered Jesus life (cf. Matt. 4), but
Jesus saw the fallacy. The selfish life is the dying life. But
he who dies to self lives unto God. Finding by losing, keeping
by giving, living by dying — in so doing the Christian mounts
the stairs to the throne. If man confesses in Christ and Christ
is to confess in him, there can be no other way.

Matthew 11

THE GREAT INVITATION

11:28. "Come unto me, all ye that labor and are heavy laden, and I will give you rest."

11:29. "Take my yoke upon you, and learn of me; for I am meek and lowly in heart: and ye shall find rest unto your souls."

11:30. "For my yoke is easy, and my burden is light."

I. HISTORICAL SETTING. The events of this chapter form a sequence: the perplexity of John; the unreasonableness of the age; the impenitent cities; the simpleminded, trusting "babes." These are the different attitudes confronting the King. He encountered them in Galilee on a given day. The chapter concludes with one of Jesus' great invitations, issued to all of these attitudes.

II. EXPOSITORY MEANING

Matt. 11:28. "Come." This is an exclamation like "come hither," and is used as an imperative, a command. "Labor" is a participle, the ones fainting from weariness. "Heavy laden." This perfect participle indicates a permanent state of weariness. "And I" is emphatic as opposed to other teachers such as the rabbis. "Give you rest" is one verb. "I will refresh or rejuvenate you."

Matt. 11:29. "Take" is an aorist imperative of point action. "Yoke." This does not relate to oxen pulling a load. "To take the yoke" was a rabbinical phrase meaning to enroll under a teacher. "Learn" is an imperative, "be taught of me." "Meek and lowly." The ancients did not regard these as virtues. "Ye shall find rest." This was sought but not found through other teachers.

Matt. 11:30. "easy." Moffatt translates this "kindly." "Burden" here is contrasted with "heavy laden" in verse 28. They are kindred words.

III. DOCTRINAL VALUE. This passage involves the experience of the Christian life from regeneration through sanctification. Man seeks a full knowledge of God only to be frustrated in his search. Jesus is the Teacher who fully understands and reveals God. His revelation is offered to all men, but is received only as they forsake worldly wisdom to become as babes in Christ.

IV. PRACTICAL AIM. To set forth the Christian experience as submission to the Teacher and application under His guidance. God is not comprehended through knowledge but through faith. That which is impossible to the "wise and prudent" becomes easy to "babes."

V. HOMILETICAL FORM

Theme: "The Great Invitation."

Introduction: This invitation is found only in Matthew, although it reflects the sensitivity of John. The Christ of the one is the Christ of the other. Jesus saw men as sheep having no shepherd (cf. Matt. 9:36). Everywhere men were searching for the better life. Underneath their doubts (Matt. 11:2 ff.), indifference (11:16 ff.), and sin (11:20 ff.) was a thirst and hunger after God. In their midst Jesus stood and called. He is doing so today. In His call is a challenge, a condition, and a promise.

A. *The Challenge* — "Come unto me . . . ."

This challenge is issued to those who "labor and are heavy laden." The former suggests active toil. The latter depicts endurance. This is a metaphor. Men seek a knowledge of God. They are burdened with a lack of this knowledge. The Greeks sought the *summum bonum* through wisdom. The Jews were burdened with ritual and works of the law. There is no labor so wearisome, no burden so heavy, as that which ends in frustration.

Jesus says, "You have sought elsewhere in vain. Come unto me . . . and I will refresh, rejuvenate you." He offers rest from the letter in the spirit, from form by reality, from conjecture by certainty, from past traditions by the present voice of God (cf. A. B. Bruce, *The Expositor's Greek Testament,* in loco).

B. *The Condition* — "Take my yoke... learn of me...."
Jesus used many figures to illustrate the Christian experience (cf. new birth, John 3, and marriage, Matt. 9:15). Here He sees it as enrolling in school (cf. disciple, pupil). The second one is born he is a child. At marriage he becomes a husband. The split second he enrolls in school, he becomes a pupil. He may be a disobedient child, a thoughtless husband, or an indolent pupil. But he is what he has become. The Christian may prove to be disappointing to God, but he is nevertheless a Christian.

Beyond the initial coming into being is a continuous becoming. In the above examples it involves growth, development, reproduction, learning, and service. No Christian can be content simply to be. He must become. He must fulfil his purpose of being. This involves justification, sanctification, and glorification. The first is a fixed condition. The degrees of the others are determined by one's application to the learning, and resultant serving, process.

C. *The Promise* — "my yoke is easy ... burden light."
This does not mean that the process involves no toil. But it is a toil of love and joy. The yoke is kindly to wear. In one sense it is the heaviest of yokes. Jesus makes strong demands. But for that reason it is light. High ideals and their accomplishment remove the sense of wearisome toil and rugged endurance. Though Jesus asks much, He provides the power to respond. Both teacher and pupil rejoice in the resultant achievements. The toil of the road will seem as nothing when one reaches the end, or goal, of the way.

Matthew 12

THE UNPARDONABLE SIN

12:24. "But when the Pharisees heard it, they said, This fellow doth not cast out devils, but by Beelzebub . . . ."

12:28. "But if I cast out devils by the Spirit of God, then the kingdom of God is come unto you."

12:31. "Wherefore I say unto you, All manner of sin and blasphemy shall be forgiven unto men: but the blasphemy against the Holy Ghost shall not be forgiven unto men."

12:32. "And whosoever speaketh a word against the Son of man, it shall be forgiven him; but whosoever speaketh against the Holy Ghost, it shall not be forgiven him, neither in this world, neither in the world to come."

I. HISTORICAL SETTING. This marks the beginning of what is called the "Busy Day" (cf. Matt. 12:22 — 13:53; Matt. 8:18-34: and parallels in Mark and Luke). It began in Galilee and continued in Gerasa, with two crossings of the sea of Galilee. The time is shortly past the middle of Jesus' public ministry, in the midst of the Great Galilean ministry.

II. EXPOSITORY MEANING

Matt. 12:24. "Pharisees." Note their increasing opposition to Jesus, due to His growing popularity, and the contrast of attitudes in verses 23-24 (cf. Mark 3:22). "This fellow." "Fellow" is not in the original Greek. Literally, "this one," showing their contempt for Jesus. "Beelzebub." The etymology of this word is difficult. Some suggestions are "lord of a dwelling," "lord of flies," "lord of dung," or "lord of idolatrous sacrifices." Some suggest a play on the name of the Canaanite god, Baal. Obviously a title of contempt applied by the Jews to Satan (cf. Matt. 12:26).

Matt. 12:28. In Matthew 12:25-29 Jesus exposes their hypocrisy and illogical statement. The focal point is verse 28. "Spirit of God" versus Satan, Jesus versus Pharisees, kingdom of God versus kingdom of evil.

Matthew 12:31. "Wherefore." Literally, "because of this." Jesus introduces a conclusion based upon verses 24-30. Note the gravity of Mark's account (3:28). "Blasphemy." This is a compound word meaning harmful or injurious speech.

Matt. 12:32. "Against the Son of man ... against the Holy Spirit." This explains verse 31. Note the contrast. "Neither ... neither ...." The Jews said blasphemy against God could be forgiven only by death. Jesus extends unforgiveness into eternity.

III. DOCTRINAL VALUE. This is the unpardonable sin. Jesus here speaks of internal attitude and its serious consequences (cf. Matt. 12:34-35). Involved is the very essence both of good and evil. Prejudice, selfishness, or malice may so cloud a man's judgment as to make, for him, evil good, and good evil. For such there is no hope.

IV. PRACTICAL AIM. To show the serious consequences of a wrong attitude toward the gospel which involves all of the gracious work of God. This includes not only those who knew Jesus in the flesh, but everyone today who responds negatively, either by denunciation or indifference, to the gospel appeal.

V. HOMILETICAL FORM
Theme: "The Unpardonable Sin."

Introduction: That a miracle had been performed the Pharisees could not deny. Before their very eyes a blind and dumb man was made to see and speak. Others saw it, and glorified God. The Pharisees saw it, and blasphemed God. There is no logical argument against evident results. One can either accept them in faith, or else reject them in wilful denial. The Pharisees chose the latter course. The response is the gravest words which ever fell from Jesus' lips. In this passage are words of blasphemy, confirmation, and condemnation.

A. *The Words of Blasphemy* — "cast out devils . . . by . . . the prince of devils."

A supernatural power had been exerted. But whose? ". . . the people were amazed . . . ." The Pharisees were contemptuous. Jesus called this latter blasphemy or the sin against the Holy Spirit.

It was a calculated sin, not one of impulse. The Pharisees' developing attitude toward Jesus may be described as curiosity, indifference, denial, maliciousness, blasphemy, and vengeance.

It was a sin of knowledge. They saw but refused to perceive. The more good Jesus did, the more they opposed Him. When they could no longer deny, they blasphemed.

It was a sin of finality. When they could no longer ignore, they rejected completely. Like John Milton's Satan, they said, "Evil, be thou my good." Jesus had no alternative but to avow their choice.

Some insist that this sin is no longer possible since Jesus is no longer on the earth. But it is not a sin against Jesus (cf. 12:31), but against the Holy Spirit who is in the earth. As such a sin it is the rejection of the very principle of good in favor of evil. In regard to the gospel message it is a final rejection of its claims upon one's soul. To do so is to regard the promised salvation as evil and the work of Satan, rather than good and the work of God. One may do so while living. To die in a state of unbelief is most certainly to do so.

B. *The Words of Confirmation* — "the kingdom of God is come unto you."

This is the inevitable conclusion of Jesus' reasoning (12:25-30). By their own words Jesus condemned the Pharisees. No one in league with Satan would cast out his servants. What about their own claims to cast out demons? How could Jesus overpower Satan if He worked by Satan's power? If, then, Jesus is destroying Satan's kingdom, He is establishing the Kingdom of God. To deny it is to deny the work of God. It is to make a calculated, conscious, and deliberate choice of evil to the rejection of the good.

The works of God continue among us. Wherever the gospel of Christ goes it changes lives and conditions. Many receive it gladly. Many reject it wilfully. One cannot be neutral where Christ is concerned. Either He works by the Spirit of God or by the spirit of Satan. To ignore Him is to reject Him. The greater the knowledge, the greater the sin.

C. *The Words of Condemnation* — "it shall not be forgiven him . . . ."

These are harsh, strange words from One who would forgive all. But there are conditions governing this forgiveness. God cannot ignore sin. He will not violate human personality.

Why did Jesus specify blasphemy against the Holy Spirit as the unpardonable sin? He allowed for differences of opinion regarding Himself. He recognized the binding power of social custom. But the Spirit of God involves every element of goodness. To reject Him is to choose evil for good. It is a fixed state. If evil becomes good, then good is evil.

B. H. Carroll offered the following explanation. If one blasphemes God the Father, there still remain the Son and Holy Spirit. If he blasphemes the Son, there is yet the Holy Spirit. But if he blasphemes the Spirit, there is none left. He has rejected deity altogether. This sin is impossible for the Christian. For the non-Christian it is the end result of a gradual, habitual, and growing enmity against God.

Matthew 13

THE CHURCH OF THE LIVING GOD

13:45. "Again, the kingdom of heaven is like unto a merchantman, seeking goodly pearls:"

13:46. "Who, when he had found one pearl of great price, went and sold all that he had, and bought it."

I. HISTORICAL SETTING. This is in the afternoon of the "Busy Day." Jesus with a series of parables, taught the multitudes by the sea of Galilee. The parable was one of Jesus' favorite methods of teaching. In all He uttered fifty-two parables. The word "parable" means a casting alongside. Jesus cast spiritual truth alongside a natural one. Someone called a parable an earthly story with a heavenly meaning. Another described a parable as a handle by which to carry a spiritual truth. The parable of the pearl of great price was spoken to the Twelve in the privacy of a home (cf. Matt. 13:36).

II. EXPOSITORY MEANING

Matt. 13:45. "kingdom of heaven." This is not to be distinguished from the "kingdom of God." A comparison of the gospels reveals that the terms are often used interchangeably. "Merchantman." This is a traveling merchant, a drummer. "Seeking." This present participle suggests continuous seeking. "Pearls." The word means purity.

Matt. 13:46. "found." This is an aorist participle expressing the excitement of the merchant at the moment of discovery. "Great price." So because it was large, round, and pure. "Went." Literally he "went away." This aorist participle expresses the immediacy and haste of the act. "Sold." The perfect tense involves a complete, final sale of all that he had accumulated in the past. "Had" is an imperfect tense

69

of continuous action in past time. "Bought." This aorist tense is point action of one definite purchase. It means to buy in the market place. The Greek tenses tell a vivid story here as elsewhere.

III. DOCTRINAL VALUE. Herein is seen the value of the Church and the price paid for it. Note the intensity of God in accomplishing it. The kingdom of heaven excels all other values.

IV. PRACTICAL AIM. To bring to the heart the truth that redemption is a gift of God's grace, not the fruit of man's works. To show how men should regard the Church of Jesus Christ.

V. HOMILETICAL FORM

Theme: "The Church of the Living God."

Introduction: A parable is intended to teach one truth, not many. To press every detail is to lose its lesson. This series of parables reveals many reflections of light from the gem of the kingdom of heaven. But the parable under consideration has to do with the kingdom itself. The kingdom of heaven is not a political entity. Nor is it outward form. It is an inner condition. It is God's rule in His universe. But specifically, in our Scripture, Jesus sees it as the rule of God in the hearts of men. It involves the merchant, the pearl, and the price.

A. *The Merchant* — "a merchant man seeking . . . ."

Here is a traveling pearl merchant going to pearl divers and markets, examining their wares, and buying the best. Who is he? Some regard him as man seeking for the kingdom of heaven. In one way or another man is seeking a Utopia. His search involves various avenues of approach, economics, politics, culture, religion. In the last of these is the hunger after God. But the Bible teaches that the initiative is with God, not man (cf. Gen. 3:9; I John 4:9-10). Man's yearning is in response to God's initiative.

The merchant is Jesus. Jesus sought throughout the universe to find the "one pearl." Finding it He did that which was necessary to procure it. The incarnation finds its meaning in this fact (cf. John 1:11-12). He sought not for Himself, but for another. The finest pearls were worn only by kings. So Jesus is seeking that which is worthy to be presented to the King, even God. Note the earnest purpose in His seeking.

B. *The Pearl* — "...one pearl...."

This pearl is so perfect in shape, pure in substance, and resplendent in beauty as to exceed all others. It is fit to be worn only by a king. The Jews did not so value the pearl, but the Gentiles did.

Jesus likened the kingdom of heaven unto this pearl. The kingdom of heaven suggests the Church of Jesus Christ, composed of all the redeemed of all ages. It is the supreme value of this age (cf. Rev. 21:2).

Jesus discerned the pearl. He found it and revealed it. The pearl is a mystery. The kingdom of heaven is a mystery. The gospel is a mystery (cf. Eph. 3:3 ff.). But its revelation is the purpose of the ages (cf. Eph. 3:11). And it finds its meaning in Christ, the Merchant, discovering and evaluating the "pearl."

C. *The Price* — "...bought it."

The merchant "went and sold all that he had, and bought it." It took all that Jesus had to purchase the "church of God" (Acts 20:28).

Note the excitement of the Merchant in His discovery (cf. Matt. 13:46, "found," aorist participle; Heb. 12:2, "for the joy..."). He "went away" from heaven to procure it. He "sold" (perfect tense, permanent, complete sale) all that He "had" (imperfect tense of continuous action in past time; cf. Phil. 2:6-8; John 17:5). He "bought" (aorist of point action, one transaction; cf. Heb. 9:12; Heb. 10:10). "Once" in both verses means "once for all" — to present to the King (cf. I Cor. 15:24-28). It shall adorn Him and enhance His glory in eternity. The Christian should do so even now.

Matthew 14

THE HUNGRY MULTITUDES

14:15. "... his disciples came unto him, saying ... send the multitude away, that they may go into the villages, and buy themselves victuals."

14:16. "But Jesus said unto them, They need not depart; give ye them to eat."

14:17. "And they say unto him, We have here but five loaves, and two fishes."

14:18. "He said, Bring them hither to me."

I. HISTORICAL SETTING. The time is just one year prior to the crucifixion (John 6:4). The place is near Bethsaida Julias (Luke 9:10) on the eastern shore of the sea of Galilee. This was in the tetrarchy of Philip, a brother of Herod Antipas. Herod Antipas' identification of Jesus as John the Baptist returned from the dead (Matt. 14:2) may have prompted Jesus' withdrawal from Galilee, Herod's domain (cf. Matt. 14:12-13). Actually this is the first of four withdrawals from Galilee during the late spring, summer, and early fall of A.D. 29. The reasons for these withdrawals probably were the enmity of Herod Antipas, the growing hostility of the Pharisees, the fanaticism of the people, the need for privacy to teach the Twelve, and the desire to escape the summer heat to rest. Note that in withdrawal Jesus keeps out of Herod's territory, and He goes each time into the mountains. The feeding of the five thousand is reported by all four gospel writers. It marked the turning point in Jesus' popularity with the people (14:22-23; cf. John 6:14-15).

II. EXPOSITORY MEANING

Matt. 14:15. "evening." This is probably the first of two

"evenings," about 3:00 P.M. "Desert." This was an out-of-the-way place with only villages nearby. "Send . . . away." This is an aorist imperative. "Send away immediately." "Go." The word renders an aorist participle, "going away immediately." Time is short. "Buy themselves." "Buy" is an aorist subjunctive, "they may buy immediately." "Themselves" is stated, and so emphatic.

Matt. 14:16. "But" contrasts Jesus' attitude with that of the disciples. "Not" is emphatic in the Greek. "Give" is an aorist imperative, the same as "send away" in verse 15. The disciples said, "Send them away." Jesus countered with "Give ye them to eat." Literally, "Give to them you to eat." Note the emphasis in "them you."

Matt. 14:17 "And" is better translated "but," with the same effect of contrast as in verse 16. In verse 14 "and" is one word (*kai*). Verses 15-18 are introduced with another word (*de*) "but." It is an adversative of contrast. "Say" is a present tense, they "keep on saying." "Loaves . . . fishes." These were thin barley cakes and little dried fishes.

Matt. 14:18. "Bring." This is an imperative, and so a command. "Them" refers to the food, not to the people.

III. DOCTRINAL VALUE. This incident bears witness to the responsibility placed upon the followers of the King. They are to feed the hungry multitudes. Note the hesitant helplessness of the disciples and the competency of Jesus.

IV. PRACTICAL AIM. To convict minds and hearts as to the failure of Christian people in their ministry to the multitudes. Jesus does not excuse them but rebukes them. Our little in Jesus' hands is enough.

V. HOMILETICAL FORM
   Theme: "The Hungry Multitudes."
Introduction: When Jesus' little boat put out to sea, the crowds, sensing His destination, ran around the northern end of the lake and met Him on the other side. In compassion He "healed their sick" (14:14). This was a miraculous ministry worked by Jesus. But the people needed another ministry. They needed to be fed. This suggests their deeper

need for spiritual food. The subsequent situation may be described as concern, hesitancy, and sufficiency.

A. *The Concern of the Twelve.* ". . . his disciples came to him . . . ."

No one can deny the genuine concern of the disciples. They shared Jesus' compassion (14:14). The people were hungry, and they wanted them fed. The place and time demanded that something be done. So they brought the problem to Jesus. But they did not ask Jesus for instructions. They instructed Jesus instead. Note the imperative verb "send . . . away." Rather than ask Jesus they commanded Him.

Christian people share a general concern for the fainting multitudes. They want them to be saved and fed. But too often they come with their own ideas rather than following the commands of God's Word. "Why doesn't God do something?" they ask. Too seldom do they ask, "What can we do?" Less seldom do they ask, "Lord what wilt thou have me to do?" The answer has already been given. But the question is not forthcoming.

B. *The Hesitancy of the Twelve.* "We have here but . . . ."
The Twelve hesitated because they failed to realize the means at their disposal. Therefore note their suggestions and Jesus' reply.

(1) ". . . send the multitude away . . . ." Away from them, away from Jesus. Let them look elsewhere for sustenance. They sought to be rid of their responsibility.

(2) " . . . that they may go into the villages . . . ." This suggests other sources of help: political, civic, cultural, economic, and psychiatric. These have their place, but they are not sufficient for man's deepest needs.

(3) ". . . buy themselves victuals." This suggests self-help apart from the ministry of Jesus or His followers.

(4) "They need not depart; give ye them to eat." At the disposal of the church of Jesus Christ is ample provision to minister to the spiritual hunger of men. The command of Jesus is that churches shall discharge their duty.

C. *The Sufficiency of Christ.* "Bring them hither to me."

What they had they brought to Jesus. By His power it was enough and more than enough (14:19-21: cf. Isa. 55:1-2).

Apart from Jesus no one is sufficient. But in Him all things are possible (cf. Phil. 4:13). One plus God is equal to every situation and need. Note the order of the service (14:19 f.). (1) They brought what they had to Jesus. (2) Jesus blessed it and apportioned it. (3) He gave the portions to the several disciples (cf. I Cor. 12). (4) The disciples gave to the people. (5) The people ate and were filled. (6) The residue exceeded even that with which they began. The more religion one gives away, the more he has.

Matthew 15

THE KINGDOM STANDARD OF VALUE

*15:2. "Why do thy disciples transgress the tradition of the
elders? for they wash not their hands when they eat bread."*

*15:3. "... Why do ye also transgress the commandment of
God by your tradition?"*

*15:11. "Not that which goeth into the mouth defileth a
man; but that which cometh out of the mouth, this defileth
a man."*

I. HISTORICAL SETTING. The time is late summer in
A.D. 29. The place is Galilee, specifically the land of Genne-
saret (Matt. 14:34), and probably in Capernaum. Jesus has
returned from the eastern side of the lake where He fed
the five thousand. The Pharisees from Jerusalem press their
opposition to Jesus. Note the growing boldness of these
critics. Already they have been joined by the Herodians (cf.
Matt. 12:14; Mark 3:6). Soon the Sadducees will join their
arch enemies in their efforts to put Jesus to death (Matt.
16:6). The differences of these three groups are resolved in
their common hatred for Jesus.

II. EXPOSITORY MEANING

Matt. 15:2. "transgress." This means to step by the side of
or deviate. The present tense suggests repeated action. They
accuse Jesus of allowing His disciples to sin. "Traditions."
This means that which was handed down by the "elders" of
the past, speaking *ex cathedra*. The reference is to the oral
law or Mishna. This washing of the hands was not for physical cleanliness, but it was a religious ritual of outward righteousness. The elders said that a demon, Shibta, sat on men's
hands while they slept. Not to wash their hands meant that
the demon was transferred to their food and thence to their

bodies. No such teaching is found in the Old Testament.

Matt. 15:3. "commandment of God." Note the contrast. Jesus accuses the Pharisees of sin in replacing God's commandment with the oral law. In their practice the latter superseded the former.

Matt. 15:11. "defileth." The word means "common." Here it is used in the bad sense of uncleanness (cf. Acts 10:14). Jesus contrasts unclean food with unclean words or attitudes. Defilement was a serious matter with the Jewish ceremonialists. This verse and following were spoken to the crowd (15:10).

III. DOCTRINAL VALUE. In this passage is contrasted ceremonial righteousness and true righteousness. A man may be outwardly correct and inwardly wrong. The traditions of man should never supersede the commandments of God.

IV. PRACTICAL AIM. To impress upon the hearers the nature of kingdom righteousness as opposed to man's righteousness. Man looks on the outward appearance, but God looks into the heart.

V. HOMILETICAL FORM

Theme: "The Kingdom Standard of Value."

Introduction: The religion of Jesus was in direct contrast with the religion of the Pharisees. His refusal to compromise His teaching to theirs figured in the crucifixion. Tradition, in the evil sense, always conflicts with spiritual religion. They are based upon two different things: the one upon the customs of man, the other upon the commandments of God. The one is outward, the other is inward. This contrast may be set forth in the words custom, conflict, and cleanliness.

A. *The Power of Custom.* "tradition of the elders . . . ."

Man is a creature of habits, customs, or traditions. These may be good (cf. I Cor. 11:2 where "ordinances" means traditions) or they may be bad (cf. Matt. 15:3). Many activities progress from act to habit to custom to tradition. Within themselves they may be good or bad. Sometimes, as here, they spring from superstition. In any segment of society these may be found. They are essentially *taboos.* Such often take on the aura of religion. In such cases they became binding to the suppression of a genuine spiritual experience. Because "everybody's doing it" does not make it right. More likely it is wrong. If tradition is the only basis of an act, even good within itself, it may rightly be questioned.

B. *The Conflict between Custom and Commandment.* "transgress the commandment of God by your tradition?"

The Bible contains many commands of God. Within themselves they are good. But when they are obeyed merely as a custom, they become bad. Satan takes good things and makes them evil. Worship as a custom only is robbed of its essential meaning. Bible reading, prayer, church membership may be viewed likewise. These are but examples of which there are many (cf. John 4:20-24; John 5:39-40).

There is always conflict between tradition for tradition's sake and the vital, spiritual meaning of God's Word. Note the custom of "Corban" (Matt. 15:4-6) and the empty practice of religion (Matt. 15:7-9). In the one God's "commandment with promise" is violated. In the other the whole of worship is nullified. Any type of stereotyped religious practice conflicts with the teachings of God's Word. Outward form is not enough. For religion to be genuine it must reach into the inner springs of the heart and will. The attitude determines the validity of the act.

C. *The True Cleanliness.* "...this defileth a man."

The Pharisees regarded that which entered a man as defiling him. Hence their tradition of washing their hands. It was not physical cleanliness but ceremonial cleanliness which concerned them. Basically it was superstition. By a simple illustration Jesus set this aside. True cleanliness is inward.

The attitude of the Pharisees still prevails (cf. Matt. 23:25-28). It is not enough to garnish and adorn the outside. Worshippers go to church or elsewhere carefully groomed, but what of the inner attitude?

That which comes out of a man reveals the inner condition (cf. Matt. 15:18-20).

Matthew 16

THE PERSON OF JESUS CHRIST

16:13. "... Whom do men say that I, the Son of man, am?"

16:15. "... But whom say ye that I am?"

16:16. "... Thou art the Christ, the Son of the living God."

I. HISTORICAL SETTING. This event came during the fourth and last withdrawal. The time is probably late September in A.D. 29. The place is near Caesarea Philippi in the region of Mount Hermon in the northern part of Palestine. This was in the tetrarchy of Herod Philip, hence the name to distinguish it from Caesarea by the sea. Literally, "Caesarea, the one of Philip." The place was originally called Paneas. It was a center of idol worship. Even today one may see the remains of such temples and altars. In this area Herod the Great had built a temple to Caesar Augustus, suggesting the worship of Caesar. Examination time had come for the Twelve. This was a perfect place for such a test.

II. EXPOSITORY MEANING
Matt. 16:13. "say." This is a present tense suggesting varied opinions of Jesus. "Son of man." This was Jesus' favorite designation of Himself. Ezekiel used it repeatedly of himself. Note Daniel 7:13. This is the probable source of this title for Jesus. It is definitely Messianic. Note that in the New Testament it is from Jesus' lips only, save John 12:34 (quoting Jesus) and Acts 7:56.
Matt. 16:15. "say ye." In the Greek "ye" is stated in the emphatic position, and also implied in the verb. Literally, "But ye, whom me do you say to be?"
Matt. 16:16. "answered." This is an aorist participle, one definite avowal. "Thou" is emphatic. It is both stated and the first word of the answer. "Christ." This is Greek for

the Hebrew "Messiah," the Anointed One. Note that in Greek there are four definite articles. Literally, "Thou art the Christ the Son of the God the living." Each article makes each of these specific. "The God the living" is in contrast with the dead gods of stone which abounded there.

III. DOCTRINAL VALUE. In this confession is found both the humanity and the deity of Jesus. The Christ is declared to be both man and God. Men's opinions may vary, but the Father's revelation is certain.

IV. PRACTICAL AIM. To present the King as one with man and one with God. In essence He is the God-man, the fulfilment of the hopes which abound in the word "Christ" or "Messiah."

V. HOMILETICAL FORM
   Theme: "The Person of Jesus Christ."
Introduction: Behind Jesus were the plaudits of the multitudes. Before Him lay the abandonment of the mobs. What is the conviction of the Twelve concerning Him? Will they be able to resist the clamor of these mobs? When they see Him forsaken, beaten, and crucified will they stand firm? The future of Christianity rests upon them. Jesus has taught them, but have they learned the lesson? Did His followers then, yea, do they now, comprehend Him and His mission? In this examination are seen popular opinion, personal conviction, and permanent value.

   A. *The Answer of Popular Opinion.* "... men say ...."
Probably the Twelve, in holiday fashion, were examining various idols and altars, identifying them one by one. Jesus interrupted their game with a question. "Whom do men say that I ... am?" They replied with varied answers. Note that they thoughtfully withheld such answers as demon and madman. Instead they mentioned the more complimentary ones: John the Baptist, Elijah, Jeremiah and other prophets. Note these as the answers of established government, institutional religion, and public surmise.

   Men saw varied things in Jesus: preaching, fire, lamentation, teaching. This is the error of putting Jesus in specific

categories. Men still emphasize one aspect of Jesus' person
to the neglect of all others. In so doing they miss the true
portrayal of His meaning and mission.

B. *The Answer of Personal Conviction.* "... whom say
ye ....?"

Peter answered for the Twelve. They saw the above elements but they saw more. Their *seeing* was not the conclusion of logic but the conviction of divine revelation (16:17).
Through intimate association they observed the many facets
of Jesus' being. Under God's guidance these added up to the
right answer. Objective and casual reason is no substitute
for a personal and abiding experience.

C. *The Essence of Permanent Value.* "... The Christ, the
Son of the living God."

Note the many facets of the King's person. (1) Son of man:
representative man, involving His earthly ministry, passion,
and second advent (cf. Matt. 8:20; 9;6; 11:19; 12:40; 17:9,
22; 20:18; 13:41; 24:27, 30). (2) Christ: eternal God, involving the eternal redemptive purpose (cf. Eph. 3:11), the Suffering Servant (cf Isaiah), the eternal Kingdom (cf. I Cor.
15:22-28). (3) Son of the living God: God in the form of
man (cf. John 1:1, 14; cf. Matt. 1:21-23). Jesus is not a dead
figure of history but the Son of the *living* God.

These abiding truths are as much needed today as in the
first century. God cares. He has invaded time for eternal
purposes. This invasion is seen in the Christ, Son of man
and Son of God. Though men may variously regard Him,
He is still the beloved Son of the living God. He is history's
origin and goal. He is man's only Saviour.

Matthew 17

THE UNIQUE SAVIOUR

17:2. "And [Jesus] was transfigured before them: and his face did shine as the sun, and his raiment was white as the light."

17:3. "And, behold, there appeared unto them Moses and Elijah talking with him."

17:5. "... This is my beloved Son, in whom I am well pleased; hear ye him."

17:8. "... they saw no man, save Jesus only."

I. HISTORICAL SETTING. It was late September, A.D. 29, just before the Feast of Tabernacles. One week after the event in Matthew 16:13 ff. (cf. Matt. 17:1; Luke 9:28), Jesus took Peter, James, and John up the slopes of Mount Hermon (cf. Mark 5:37; Matt. 26:37). There Jesus was transfigured. After the confession of Matthew 16:16 Peter, and the rest, demonstrated their lack of comprehension as to the cross (Matt. 16:21-23) which was only six months away. Gloom once again settled upon Jesus. G. Campbell Morgan sees a note of estrangement between Jesus and the Twelve during this week. The Transfiguration was given for the benefit of both.

II. EXPOSITORY MEANING

Matt. 17:2. "transfigured." The Greek word is "metamorphosed." It means a change of form. See Romans 12:2 for this word ("be ye transformed"). Note also II Corinthians 3:18. It is used of the shining of Moses' face ("metamorphosed from glory unto glory" cf. Mark 9:2-3; Luke 9:29).

Matt. 17:3. "Moses and Elijah." They are symbols of law and prophecy, the Old Testament revelation. With Jesus, note law, prophecy, and grace. Both Moses and Elijah left

this world under extraordinary circumstances. "Talking."
This is a present participle of repeated action or conversation. Luke 9:31 says that they talked "of his decease" or
exodus (literally) from this world. This includes His death,
resurrection, and ascension.

Matt. 17:5. "bright cloud." Such clouds form quickly over
Mount Hermon. "Bright" suggests the Shekinah glory or
God's presence (cf. Num. 9:15). "My beloved Son...."
This is the same confirmation given at Jesus' baptism (Matt.
3:17). "Hear ye him," even when He speaks of His death.
It is a sharp rebuke to Peter and the others. "Hear" is a
present imperative, a command. "Keep on hearing him."

Matt. 17:8. "no man, save Jesus only." Literally, "no one
they saw except Jesus only." Moses and Elijah were gone.
Only Jesus remained.

III. DOCTRINAL VALUE. In this passage is seen the su-
premacy of the King. He alone can save, and that through
His "exodus." The old revelation is swallowed up in the
new. Jesus stands alone in the arena of redemption as both
God and man. It is sinful to align Him with any other.

IV. PRACTICAL AIM. To point out Jesus as perfect God
and perfect man fulfilling God's redemptive purpose. All
others must give place to Him. Regardless of men's opinion
of Him, He is still well-pleasing to God.

V. HOMILETICAL FORM

Theme: "The Unique Saviour."

Introduction: Jesus had reached the point of no return.
If the disciples did not understand, Jesus did, and so did
heaven. Behind Jesus is the desertion by the multitudes.
Present is the density of the Twelve. Before Him is the *Via
Dolorosa* to the cross. But events of recent days had clouded
the issue. Six months before the crucifixion the disciples are
not ready for the event. Once again Satan tries to swerve
Jesus from the cross (cf. Matt. 16:23). As God Jesus knows
the future. As man He is momentarily discouraged. The
Transfiguration was for His benefit as well as that of the
Twelve. This event may be summarized as transfiguration,
conversation, and confirmation.

A. *The Transfiguration of Jesus.* "... transfigured before them ...."

In the Transfiguration Jesus appears as both man and God. As man He had a form, wore raiment, and experienced discouragement. As God He was *metamorphosed*. The light was not from without. It was His deity shining forth from within. G. Campbell Morgan says that the wick of His essential deity was suddenly turned up. He was the perfect man. Had He been less, this sudden outrushing of deity would have killed him.

Here is perfect deity and perfect humanity, the God-man. As He was glorified in the "throe of Calvary," so was He glorious in "the glow of Hermon." Here one sees "the glory as of the only begotten of the Father" (John 1:14).

B. *The Conversation of the Saviour and the Servants.* "... Moses and Elijah talking with him."

Elsewhere in moments of stress angels ministered to Jesus (cf. Matt. 4:11; Luke 22:43). Why not here? Why Moses and Elijah? Note the relationships of Moses, Elijah, and Jesus: Sinai, Carmel, Calvary respectively; Moses (law), Elijah (prophecy), Jesus (grace). The first two found fulfilment in the third. Moses and Elijah were symbolic of the Old Covenant; Jesus symbolizes the New Covenant. Moses and Elijah epitomize the Old Testament saints who were saved, on credit, looking in faith toward the Christ.

Why did they speak of Jesus' "exodus"? It involved that which Jesus should do for the salvation of all men who trusted in Him. It involved law, sin, and grace. Angels as a-moral beings could not comprehend these things. Hence Moses and Elijah. What did they say to Jesus? They affirmed heaven's plan. If Jesus' exodus were not completed, those who had died in faith would not be saved. Heaven would be emptied and hell filled. Encouraged, Jesus "stedfastly set his face to go to Jerusalem" (Luke 9:51).

C. *The Confirmation of the Father.* "... my beloved Son ... hear ye him ... Jesus only."

Peter broke into the conversation to propose three tabernacles. It was near the time for the Feast of Tabernacles.

The "mountain-top experience" was glorious. Why end it?

But God's voice interrupted man's thoughts and plans. He rebuked Peter. For his desire to stay in the mountain away from need and suffering? Yes. Too many remain on Hermon to avoid Calvary. But there was more, and particularly so. Peter placed Jesus, Moses, and Elijah on the same plane. This was, and is, sin. Moses and Elijah must fade. But Jesus remains. They are to hear Jesus, not Moses and Elijah, as God's full and final revelation. What Jesus says they are to believe and do. The law or the prophets cannot save. "Jesus only" is the hope of the world. He went through His "exodus" to that end. When "Moses and Elijah" are put in their proper perspective, men see "no man, save Jesus only." This was the needed message of their day — and of every day.

Matthew 18

THE STANDARD OF KINGDOM GREATNESS

18:1. "Who [then] is the greatest in the kingdom of heaven?"

18:3. "Except ye be converted, and become as little children, ye shall not enter into the kingdom of heaven."

18:4. "Whosoever therefore shall humble himself as this little child, the same is greatest in the kingdom of heaven."

I. HISTORICAL SETTING.

From Mount Hermon Jesus returned to Capernaum. On the return trip Jesus had repeated His word about the coming crucifixion. The disciples finally understood, and "were exceeding sorry" (Matt. 17:22-23). In Capernaum they were probably in Peter's home (Matt. 17:24-27). Chapters 18-20 involve Jesus' teaching of the Twelve, both in Galilee and on His last journey to Jerusalem. John records an intermediate visit to Jerusalem (John 8-10) which is corroborated by Luke (9:51 — 13:21).

II. EXPOSITORY MEANING

Matt. 18:1. "Who [then] is greatest...?" "Then" is absent from the KJV, but appears in the best manuscripts. "Then" refers back to the events contained in Matthew 16:16-17, 27. Mark and Luke note a discussion among the Twelve as to position in the kingdom (Mark 9:33-34; Luke 9:46). Jesus' teaching (Matt. 16:21; 18:22-23), plus the consideration shown to Peter, James, and John, had upset their fixed ideas about the kingdom order of prominence.

Matt. 18:3. "ye be converted." This is an aorist passive subjunctive. It expresses a condition unfulfilled but possible of fulfilment. The action is something done to them one time by another. The verb means to turn about and is akin in

89

meaning to the Greek word for "repent," a change of mind or attitude.

Matt. 18:3. "become." This is a second aorist middle subjunctive with the same condition as above. The middle voice suggests something done to themselves. The verb basically means to come into being. The aorist tense suggests the definite beginning. These words "converted" and "become" may be called justification and sanctification respectively.

Matt. 18:3. "little children." Maybe the "child" was Peter's. Here Jesus passes from the child to those who are "converted" and "become." "Ye shall not enter." In the Greek this verb is preceded by a strong, emphatic double negative.

Matt. 18:4. "humble himself." This verb means to depress one's pride. A. B. Bruce *(The Expositor's Greek Testament)* calls this "the most difficult thing in the world for saint as for sinner."

III. DOCTRINAL VALUE. This chapter relates the true nature of the kingdom of heaven and its citizens. It reveals kingdom standards in contrast to earthly standards. Conversion is the prime requisite for citizenship, and proper development is necessary for achieving greatness in the kingdom of heaven.

IV. PRACTICAL AIM. To impress upon the hearer the false standard of greatness in contrast with Christ's standard and the consequences of each. The latter calls for a turning back and a new beginning. Both involve man's submission and God's power.

V. HOMILETICAL FORM

Theme: "The Standard of Kingdom Greatness."

Introduction: The Twelve were products of their age. They envisioned Christ's kingdom as one of pomp, power, and splendor. But they are no isolated group. Despite Jesus' teachings to the contrary their standard of values has plagued Christendom through the ages. It does so today, not only in hierarchical systems but in every local church. The example of the little child is needed perhaps more today than in the first century. It is certainly as difficult to follow. Indeed, apart from the Spirit of God it is impossible. In this chapter are seen contrast, conflict, and consequences.

A. *The Contrasting Standards.* "Who [then] is the greatest...? ...as this little child, the same is greatest...."

The disciples were having a rough time. Their dreams of glory had been shattered by Jesus' words about His death. The consideration shown to Peter, James, and John apparently did not help the situation. The failure with respect to the demon-possessed child punctured their egos. The tax-collector only aggravated the situation as he singled out Peter to the neglect of the others. If their concept of greatness was wrong "who then is greatest...?"

Note the paradox in Jesus' acted parable. He called a little child, probably playing nearby and oblivious to their problem. Here was the symbol of kingdom greatness. Note the characteristics of a child: comparative innocence, simplicity, forgiving, trusting, and possessed of almost infinite possibilities.

Furthermore note the words in verse 3 — "be converted, and become...." From their selfish adult attitudes they must return to the attitudes of childhood. This involves the new birth. From there they must "become." This suggests the process of sanctification (cf. Matt. 11:28-30; Eph. 4:13). Such greatness is the result of human submission and consecration plus divine power (cf. Phil. 2:12-13).

B. *The Conflicting Standards.* "Whosoever therefore shall humble himself...."

This is "the most difficult thing in the world for saint as for sinner." It involves conflict. (1) Within one's self as to the standard of values. Note the value of a child (18:6, 10) and of one lamb (18:12-14). See further the conflict between physical and spiritual well-being. (18:8-9). By oriental hyperbole Jesus drives home His point. (2) Within one's relations with other church members (18:15-20). Note that Jesus Himself is present as the Mediator (18:20). (3) With respect to forgiveness (18:21 ff.). A child soon forgets and forgives. Peter thought he was generous. The Rabbis required only three times, Peter suggested seven. Note Jesus' answer which amounts to infinity. Only a "converted" and *becoming* man can resolve these conflicts. This chapter is a commentary on Matthew 16:24-25.

C. *The Consequences of Failure.* "Except."

To do less than "be converted" is to miss the kingdom altogether. Not to "become" is to miss its greatness. Only a childlike spirit can receive a "child," which is to receive Christ (18:5-6). Physical death or maiming is to be preferred to missing this spirit (18:6-9). Not to show the childlike spirit of forgiveness is to suggest that one is not "converted" (18:17, 34-35). One may be a child, yet not develop the childlike spirit. Hence the importance of *becoming*. It is not realized in a day. But it can be begun in a split second. The *becoming* is the work of a lifetime.

Matthew 19

THE DEMAND OF THE KING

19:16. "And, behold, one came and said unto him, Good Master, what good thing shall I do, that I may have eternal life?"

19:20. "The young man saith unto him, All these things have I kept from my youth up: what lack I yet?"

19:22. "But when the young man heard that saying, he went away sorrowful: for he had great possessions."

I. HISTORICAL SETTING. On His final journey to Jerusalem Jesus is in Perea, "the coasts of Judea beyond Jordan" (Matt. 19:1). He was following the customary route from Galilee to Jerusalem. The Jews crossed the Jordan to avoid Samaria. It is the spring of A.D. 30, just a matter of days before the crucifixion. As Jesus journeys He ministers along the way.

II. EXPOSITORY MEANING
Matt. 19:16. "one came." The "one" is identified by Luke as a ruler (18:18). According to Matthew 19:22 he was also rich. He was a Jew prominent in position, possessions, and purity.

Matt. 19:16. "Master." This is the word *teacher*, like schoolmaster. "Good" is not in the best manuscripts of Matthew, but is genuine in Mark and Luke. They probably report the full salutation.

Matt. 19:16. "what good thing." Literally, "what good shall I do?" Verse 17 indicates that Jesus regarded his concept of "good" as inadequate. He thought of outward goodness as did the Pharisees.

Matt. 19:16. "may have eternal life." The verb is an ingressive aorist, "may come to have" or "acquire." "Eternal life" is "life of the ages" or "age-abiding life."

Matt. 19:20. "young man." This Greek word refers to one in the prime of life. "All these things" refer to the Ten Commandments. He had observed them faithfully.

Matt. 19:20. "what lack I yet?" The word "lack" means to fall short or to be defective. What more could he do than external things? A. T. Robertson suggests either proud complacency or pathetic despair. It was probably some of both.

Matt. 19:22. "sorrowful." Mark says "his countenance fell." Luke says that he was "exceedingly grieved." He went away grieved. Perhaps he thought that Jesus asked too much. "Great possessions." This could mean property or real estate. His high hopes lay in the dust.

III. DOCTRINAL VALUE. The point here is external righteousness versus internal righteousness. A person may be outwardly correct but inwardly wrong. There is a difference between negative and positive goodness. One may observe the letter of the law, yet break the spirit of it. Basic sin is in the inner attitude, not merely in the overt act.

IV. PRACTICAL AIM. To impress the hearer with the fact that Jesus' demands go beyond rote observance of religious rules. Such cannot satisfy the deepest longings of the soul. There can be no reservation in following the King. That which comes between a man and Jesus is his god.

V. HOMILETICAL FORM
   Theme: "The Demand of the King."

Introduction: Apart from the crucifixion scene there is scarcely a more pathetic picture in the Gospels than this. A young man in the prime of life came to Jesus expectantly, yet went away disappointed. He came with a smiling face, and went away with a fallen countenance. He rushed up to Jesus with a joyful heart, yet went away exceedingly sorrowful. One may well ask why. For this scene has been repeated times without number. The story may be described as hope, emptiness, and despair.

   A. *The Hope of Youth.* ". . . that I may have eternal life?"

Hope is characteristic of vigorous, ambitious, idealistic youth. It was especially true of this young man. He was rich, prominent, promising, and pure. What a life to bring to Jesus! "And Jesus looking upon him loved him . . ." (Mark 10:21).

But these things were not enough. He wanted age-abiding life. What the words "eternal life" meant to him one cannot say with certainty. But surely there was an intangible idealism which longed for realization. His concept of goodness was far short of Jesus' goal (Matt. 19:17). He thought of goodness as quantitative instead of qualitative. Jesus did not rebuke him for it, but sought to lead him to a full understanding of it. Jesus never quenches a smoking flax, but endeavors to fan it into a flame. This is the *hope* of the hope of youth.

B. *The Emptiness of Youth.* ". . . what lack I yet?"

Despite his outwardly pure life, he was not satisfied. There was a defect in his life which a mere keeping of the commandments could not mend. His life was an empty shell, perfect on the outside but hollow on the inside.

Note again the things possessed by this young man: youth, wealth, authority, position, character, idealism. Yet his life was empty. It fell short of its possibilities.

Modern youth may well study this picture. With so much of the tangibles, youth often lacks in the realization of the intangibles. The greatest youth problem is not deliquency. It is frustration. The average youth possesses idealism far beyond that of his elders. His problem lies in the fulfilment of this hunger for a better life. Lacking the proper guidance or example from their elders, they end up in the blind alley of cynicism. The unsettled state of world affairs leaves youth in a quandary. So many say, "What's the use?" But despite everything else, this young man still cherished his ideals. When youth loses them all is lost. The greatest need of youth is a noble, spiritual purpose.

C. *The Despair of Youth.* ". . . he went away sorrowful . . . ."

Why did he go away? "For he had great possessions." Not merely because he had them, but because they had him (cf. Luke 12:20). Jesus made demands upon him which he was not willing to meet. Although he claimed to have kept all the commandments, actually he had broken the first one. His possessions were his god (cf. James 2:10). This teaching of Jesus does not necessarily call for a vow of poverty. Instead it calls for a right use of property. In effect Jesus told the young man to get rid of that which stood between him and a right relationship with God and His will. The King demands absolute love and obedience.

Jesus does not command every person to sell his property and give the receipts away. It may be other things. A dime can be held so close to one's eye as to shut out the entire landscape. Whatever shuts out God must be removed. It may be intellect, doubt, pride, prejudice, cynicism, companions, occupants, or leisure. Each must examine his own life.

Because the young man was wedded to his possessions, he went away from Jesus. "...he went away sorrowful..." — but he went away. No further record of him is found. One may hope that he returned to Jesus. But all that the Bible says of him is that he sought to save his life here-and-now, and in the process lost the age-abiding life. His despair should warn others. Thus it will become their hope and assurance.

Matthew 20

A STUDY IN GREATNESS

20:25. *"But Jesus called them unto him, and said, Ye know that the princes of the Gentiles exercise dominion over them, and they that are great exercise authority upon them."*

20:26. *"But it shall not be so among you: but whosoever will be great among you, let him be your minister."*

20:27. *"And whosoever will be chief among you, let him be your servant."*

20:28. *"Even as the Son of man came not to be ministered unto, but to minister, and to give his life a ransom for many."*

I. HISTORICAL SETTING. Jesus was moving ever closer to Jerusalem and the cross. This burden weighed heavily upon Him. The event under consideration occurred probably in Perea, shortly before Jesus crossed the Jordan river near Jericho. Repeated incidents had served to focus attention upon the demands of the King. In response the Twelve inquired as to the reward; Jesus thought in terms of service. This is ever the conflict between human and divine standards. The request of James and John, through their mother, and the indignation of the other disciples, served to bring the matter into focus.

II. EXPOSITORY MEANING

Matt. 20:25. "them." This refers primarily to James and John, but includes the other disciples. "Know" is more than experiential knowledge. It involves inner perception. "Princes." They are those in places of rulership. This is a contrast with the disciples' request (20:21). "Gentiles" are pagan people. "Exercise dominion." The verb means to lord it over one. In the Greek it is an intensive form. "Great."

Literally, "the great ones or grandees." "Exercise authority" means "to play the tyrant." Another intensive form. The Greek word means authority out of the nature of one's being, with no outside restrictions. Its root form is used of God's power (cf. Matt. 28:18).

Matt. 20:26. "not." This word is first in the Greek sentence, so emphatic. "Among you" in contrast with pagan rulers. "Great among you" in contrast with "great ones" of verse 25. "Minister." This is the word for deacon *(diakonos)*. Thayer forms this word out of *dia* (through) and *konis* (dust), one who raises dust in hurrying to minister. More frequently it applies to ministers of the gospel (cf. I Cor. 3:5).

Matt. 20:27. "chief." Literally "first." "Servant." This is the word for bond slave. Note the contrast of highest and lowest dignity.

Matt. 20:28. "came not." In Greek "not" is first, and so emphatic. The very purpose of Jesus' coming. "Ministered unto, but to minister." These verbs are the root of *diakonos* (minister). The first is passive; the second is active. Both are aorist tenses of point action, referring to the whole of Jesus' ministry. "Ransom." This word was used in the papyri for the price paid for a slave in order to set him free. Some see difficulty in the suggestion that God had to pay Satan a ransom. Not so. God paid the ransom to Himself (cf. Rom. 3:23-26). This is Jesus' only use of the word (cf. parallel in Mark 10:45).

III. DOCTRINAL VALUE. Here is the contrast between worldly and heavenly standards of greatness. Service is the criterion of true grandeur. The perfect standard is Jesus Christ. He went through the cross to the throne.

IV. PRACTICAL AIM. To enable the hearer to see that one's service is more to be regarded than one's servants as an estimate of Kingdom position. Christ, not human rulers, is the pattern for successful Christian living. Faithfulness unto the point of dying should be the goal of every follower of Christ. Service, not selfishness, is the goal.

V. HOMILETICAL FORM

Theme. "A Study in Greatness."

Introduction: The very air was charged with expectancy. The words and mood of Jesus indicated a rapidly approaching climax to His ministry. Naturally the Twelve related this to the establishing of the Kingdom. Still unable to identify it with the cross, they thought in terms of some divine fiat from which would emerge the rule of Christ. This concept resulted in a scramble for positions of privilege. Maybe relying upon natural kinship, John and James, through their mother, waxed bold to request places of first and second power next to Jesus. Resentment flared through the others. Once again the patience of Jesus was sorely tried. Another lesson was in order. It may be outlined with three words: false, true, ideal.

A. *The False Standard of Greatness.* "the princes of the Gentiles . . . ."

The pagan world placed great emphasis upon "the great ones," lords and tyrants. The political scene reeked with avarice, greed, oppression, and power. From Caesar down to the local petty officials one standard prevailed, lording it over or playing the tyrant. Felix, a liberated slave, was said to exercise the power of a king with the disposition of a slave (cf. Acts 23:24 ff.) .

The Twelve were obsessed with the same idea. They thought in terms of an earthly kingdom with its hierarchy of power. Such an idea has plagued Christianity through the ages. Like a poisonous fog it hovers over every denomination, church, and individual Christian. The thirst for prominence and power nullifies Christian usefulness and negates spiritual power. Political standards and materialistic measures have no place in spiritual endeavors. Jesus forever separated them (cf. Matt. 22:21) . What God has put asunder, man should never join together.

B. *The True Standard of Greatness.* ". . . not be so among you . . . let him be your minister."

With one emphatic negative Jesus brushed aside the false to emphasize the true. Lords and tyrants have no place in the Kingdom of God. The standard of Kingdom greatness is service. Not the number of one's servants but the number whom one serves is the Christian criterion. Note the contrast: "great ... minister ... chief ... servant." The servant is a slave. The minister is a slave hastening to serve. Pagan society may scorn, but God is well pleased.

Position in the Kingdom is to be neither asked nor demanded. It is achieved and deserved. God is sovereign in giving His rewards (cf. Matt. 20:1-16). Man is free to fail or achieve. God has "proposed" greatness for those who fit themselves for it (cf. Matt. 20:23). In losing his life for Christ's sake man finds it in Christ's service. The highest plaudit is not the acclaim of the crowd, but the "well done" of the Christ. The final verdict is not one's fame or fortune, but "What did you do with Jesus?"

C. *The Ideal Standard of Greatness.* "... the Son of man ...."

"Let this mind be in you ...." (Phil. 2:5-11). King of kings and Lord of lords — yet He became a servant raising dust in His haste to serve. He trod the dusty road that led even to the cross. Herein is the explanation of the incarnation. He became everything that man is, that man might become, everything that He is. He bore man's grief that man might bear other's burdens, and "so fulfil the law of Christ" (cf. Gal. 6:2). One standard of judgment is the Christian's service toward others. (cf. Matt. 25:31-46; Luke 16:8.)

Matthew 21

WHO IS THIS?

21:10. "And when he was come into Jerusalem, all the city was moved, saying, Who is this?"

21:11. "And the multitude said, This is Jesus the prophet of Nazareth of Galilee."

I. HISTORICAL SETTING.
This is Palm Sunday, just five days before the crucifixion. It has been called Jesus' triumphant entry into Jerusalem. In fact it was His last appeal to the city. It was a further fulfilment of prophecy (21:4-5). Here the King offered Himself only to be rejected. Such entries were common in that day. A victorious king entered his capital city riding on a white stallion. Jesus, in meekness and peace, rode upon an ass, a beast of burden. Expectancy was in the air. Those who accompanied Jesus hailed Him as the Messiah (21:9). Doubtless many who cried "hosanna" on Sunday cried "crucify him" on Friday. This demonstration created a sensation among residents of the city and the pilgrims who had come for the Passover.

II. EXPOSITORY MEANING
Matt. 21:10. "moved." This means stirred as by an earthquake or a mighty wind. This is an aorist passive verb from which comes the word "seismograph" (cf. Matt. 27:51; Matt. 28:4). "Who is this?" A question of curiosity, but more. "Who is this to whom you ascribe messianic titles?"

Matt. 21:11. The answer literally reads, "This one is the prophet Jesus, the one from Nazareth of Galilee." Bruce sees this as an answer of pride. Chrysostom regarded it as "a low-pitched answer ... as if they were ashamed of their recent outburst of enthusiasm" (Bruce).

Matt. 21:11. "Jesus." To them this was a common name. Note that they did not say "Christ." "Prophet." His vocation, but just one among many. "Nazareth." A despised town of Galilee (cf. John 1:46). "Galilee." Regarded with scorn by the Judeans (cf. John 7:52-53).

III. DOCTRINAL VALUE. This question involves the entire scope of the person and work of Jesus Christ. It echoes the hunger of men's minds and hearts. The answer is the tragedy of failure in Christian witness. Truth watered down is no truth at all.

IV. PRACTICAL AIM. To impress upon the friends of Jesus the necessity of a bold, complete witness as to the person and purpose of the King. Because those who know Jesus best fail to reveal Him at His best, opportunity is lost. Furthermore cities, nations, and souls are lost.

V. HOMILETICAL FORM
   Theme: "Who Is This?"
   Introduction: What a scene! It began with hope but ended in despair. It was born in witness but was buried in denial. What promised to be a coronation became a crucifixion. Jerusalem's greatest hour soon became her final hour.

The time and place may change, but the principles are ever the same. No nation or man can confront Jesus and ever be the same again. Different people see different things in Jesus. The Roman soldiers saw the scene. A triumphant procession? No king, stallion, army, or trophies of victory. Instead a lowly man, a beast of burden, and a laughing, shouting mob. "Who is this?" they asked. The Jews saw a procession. Messianic shouts, torn garments, broken palm branches, and Galilean peasants? "Who is this?" they asked. The scene involves a question, an answer, and an examination.

   A. *The Question.* "Who is this?"
   It was an honest question. Few residents of Jerusalem knew Jesus by sight. The pilgrims probably did not know Him at all. This fact, plus natural curiosity, produced the question. In their hearts was a hunger for the Messiah. The Passover was regarded as a possible time for His manifestation. Perhaps this was He.

This question, uttered or silent, is in every heart. Though

He is the desire of all nations, many do not know Him, indeed
have never heard of Him. This question is seen in the un-
rest of men and nations. It is involved in the attempts of art,
science, culture, even theology to meet the manifold hungers
of men everywhere. Jesus Christ is the mystery of all myster-
ies. He is the answer to every need. Hence the repeated question, "Who is this?"

B. *The Answer.* ". . . Jesus the prophet of Nazareth of Galilee."

Before an eager audience this answer was a tragedy. There
were many men called Jesus, and many prophets. Nazareth
was a despised village. "No prophet came from Galilee," said
they. In effect, the crowd replied, "He's a nobody." So they
melted away, only to reassemble to cry, "Crucify him!"

The answer was true. But there was so much more truth
which they did not speak. They said nothing of the "Christ."
Outside the city He was the "Son of David." Intimidated by
the cynical city they said, "He is Jesus." To modern man that
is definite. To them it said nothing.

This tragedy is repeated daily. In the heart He is the
Christ. In the outward expression He is a nobody. Business,
pleasure, politics, scholarship, and fear of scorn are only a
few of the reasons why the friends of Jesus give the wrong
answer. They lose their opportunity. What is worse — others
lose their souls.

C. *The Examination.* "Who is this?"

The question is repeated. History, art, literature, architec-
ture, music, poetry, prose, philosophy, and psychology have
sought to answer it. But each falls short of its goal. The answer is found in the Bible. It is God's answer to man's question: (1) pre-existent (John 1:1); eternal (Heb. 13:8); divine
(John 1:1; Luke 4:9; John 17:11); Creator (John 1:3, Col.
1:16-17); virgin-born (Matt. 1:21-23); sinless (John 8:46;
Matt. 27:4; Luke 23:14; II Cor. 5:21); wonderful (Matt. 4:23;
Mark 1:22; John 7:16; 11:1-46); vicariously died (Isa. 53:4-6;
II Cor. 5:21); resurrected (Matt. 28:5-6); ascended (Acts
1:9); returning (Acts 1:11). The true answer is not merely
historical but personal. "What think ye of Christ?" (Matt.
22:42).

Matthew 22

A CITIZEN OF TWO WORLDS

22:17. "Tell us therefore, What thinkest thou? Is it lawful to give tribute unto Caesar, or not?"

22:20. "And he saith unto them, Whose is this image and superscription?"

22:21. "They say unto him, Caesar's. Then saith he unto them, Render therefore unto Caesar the things which are Caesar's; and unto God the things that are God's."

I. HISTORICAL SETTING. It was later in the day on Tuesday. The Herodians, along with the disciples of the Pharisees, came to Jesus with a tricky political question. Both groups, while differing in their politics, were opposed to the Roman rule. They objected to Roman taxation. The Pharisees sought a return to the theocratic nation. The Herodians advocated the return of kingship to the house of Herod. Had Jesus sided with them He would have brought the wrath of Rome upon Him. Had He advocated Roman taxes, the people would have turned upon Him. The question actually turned upon Roman law and Messianic law. According to their concept the latter forbade the former. To have rejected the latter would, in their eyes, have been to renounce His Messianic claims. Jesus supported neither side of the question, but spoke an eternal truth as to the relationship between Church and State.

II. EXPOSITORY MEANING

Matt. 22:17. "lawful." The reference is to theocratic or Herodian rule versus Roman rule. "Tribute" was a head tax or *tributum capitis* paid with a silver coin. "Caesar." The reigning Caesar was Tiberius who reigned A.D. 14-37.

In the larger sense "Tiberius" refers to government as an institution.

Matt. 22:20. "image and superscription." A Roman coin with Caesar's image on one side and the inscription *"Tiberiou Kaisaros"* on the other.

Matt. 22:21. — "render." This is an aorist imperative of the verb to give back or to recompense. It was a term for paying tribute money. Literally, "the things belonging to Caesar ... the things belonging to God."

III. DOCTRINAL VALUE. This is the basic word as to the relationship between Church and State. It shows the Christian's obligation to both. Implied is the higher obligation owed to God. When both Church and State recognize their respective places in God's plan, there need be no conflict.

IV. PRACTICAL AIM. To set forth the proper attitude of Kingdom citizens toward the Kingdom of God and varying political systems under which they live. To attempt to resolve the conflict in divided loyalties. Jesus had little, almost nothing, to say about politics. He dealt with guiding principles.

V. HOMILETICAL FORM
   Theme: "A Citizen of Two Worlds."
Introduction: Although the Herodians and the Pharisees' disciples acted with an ulterior motive (22:18), they posed a problem which calls for serious consideration. How can a person be a citizen of the Kingdom of God and a citizen of an earthly kingdom at the same time? Does the Chirstian conscience conflict with one's civic duties? If so, where does his loyalty lie? The truth is that he is a citizen of two worlds. In each he has responsibilities. He cannot be a good Christian and a bad citizen. Nor may the reverse be true. In dealing with this matter three words are noted: conflict, consequence, and complement.
   A. *The Conflict.* "Is it lawful...?"
Behind this *loaded* question was a real conflict. Should the advocates of a theocracy submit to pagan rule? Could the champions of Herod be subject to Caesar? The problem was both religious and political.

This is especially true for the Christian. Does loyalty to Christ precede obedience to law? Should the Church control the State, or the State the Church? Are religion and politics to be mixed? When the State makes demands contrary to religious conscience, what must the Christian do? Are extreme positions in either case ever justified? Is there a possibility of resolving these conflicts?

B. *The Consequence.* ". . . this image and superscription?" Jesus did not answer with a coin of His own or of His disciples. He asked for their coin. It was not Jewish but Roman. Its use implied their subservience to and dependence upon the Roman government. Jesus neither condoned nor condemned the Empire and its rule. He simply recognized an evident fact.

Christianity exists under many varied forms of government. The New Testament approves the institution of government (cf. Rom. 13:1 ff.). Christians are exhorted to be law abiding (cf. I Peter 2:12-17). Even when persecuted they are to endure it willingly as a testimony unto the Lord (cf. I Peter 3:14-15).

The Christian is a part of society in which he lives. He is not to live a monastic life, but is to flavor life with his witness (cf. I Cor. 5:9-13). Where laws are wrong he is to use his influence to change them. But he is to abide by them, unless they involve a matter of Christian conscience (cf. Acts 4:19-20). Always he is to be a Christian (I Peter 3:15).

C. *The Complement.* ". . . unto Caesar . . . unto God . . . ." Jesus sided with neither question. Instead He declared a principle of conduct. Some things belong to Caesar, others to God. Each is to be rendered in its own sphere. The Christian is a citizen of two worlds. Each entails obligations.

In Jesus' answer is the ideal. Neither State nor Church is bodily to control the other. In this ideal neither should fear the other. They complement each other. (cf. Rom. 13:5-10). It is under such an ideal that both State and Church have realized their greatest potential.

Matthew 23

THE JUDGMENT OF GOD

23:2. "The scribes and Pharisees sit in Moses' seat."

23:3. "All therefore whatsoever they bid you observe, that observe and do; but do not ye after their works: for they say, and do not."

23:13. "But woe unto you, scribes and Pharisees, hypocrites! . . ."

23:38. "Behold, your house is left unto you desolate."

I. HISTORICAL SETTING. This event occurred probably about mid-afternoon on Tuesday of Passion Week. It climaxed the "day of controversy." The place was probably in the court of the temple. Already Jesus had denounced the Pharisees (Luke 11:42 ff.) . Here the denunciation is completed. These are the most scathing words which ever fell from the lips of Jesus. Some have criticized Jesus for lack of self-control. But this ignores the elements involved. Through this outburst of righteous indignation runs a sobbing compassion (cf. 22:37) . Here are seen both sides of the nature of Deity, compassion and wrath.

G. Campbell Morgan notes an interesting comparison between "blessed" in Matthew 5 and "woe" in Matthew 23 (*The Gospel According to Matthew,* Revell, *in loco*). There are seven beatitudes, excepting the double beatitude in Matthew 5:10-11 (cf. 23:34-36) . There are also seven woes. Verse 14 is not found in the best manuscripts. But note parallels in Mark 12:40 and Luke 20:47.

II. EXPOSITORY MEANING

Matt. 23:2. "Moses' seat." They were regarded as the interpreters of the Mosaic law.

Matt. 23:3. "whatsoever they bid." The Mosaic law, not their multitude of rote rules of conduct. "Say, and do not." These are present tenses. "They keep on saying, and keep on not doing."

Matt. 23:13. "woe." This is an interjection. With the definite article it means "calamity" (cf. Rev. 9:12; Rev. 11:14). "Hypocrites." This word is the transliteration of a word meaning "play actor," one who plays a part. Note that it was spoken not to outward sinners but to pretenders after righteousness void of inward character.

Matt. 23:38. "house." Probably a triple meaning: temple, city, and nation. "Left desolate." This verb means to send away or dismiss. The passive form means to desert, depart from, to leave alone. Jesus gave up on the Jewish nation. In A.D. 70 judgment will fall!

III. DOCTRINAL VALUE. This chapter sets forth in frightening fashion the wrath of God against sin. It teaches the compassion of God for the sinner. Here is seen the "righteousness of the scribes and Pharisees" (cf. Matt. 5:20) or hypocrisy, the most condemned of all sins. Jesus authenticates the Mosaic code, but abhors its misuse.

IV. PRACTICAL AIM. To point out the judgment of God upon man's righteousness which ignores the righteousness of God in Christ. God is a God of wrath as well as a God of grace. The judgment of God is not an arbitrary one. He only recognizes the evil character produced. When such is fixed even God Himself can only declare it. It is left desolate.

V. HOMILETICAL FORM
Theme: "The Judgment of God."

Introduction: If Matthew 23 seems harsh, it is just that. To understand it properly one must view it against the backdrop of the preceding chapters. The King had patiently sought the Jewish nation. The more He pleaded with them the greater their rebellion. It was only after every means had failed that Jesus pronounced judgment. This is always God's way. Patience, love, mercy, compassion, and grace, when scorned, can only rebound in judgment. Such lies at the very basis of the moral structure of the universe. Man reaps what he sows. Herein is a lesson for every man. It suggests commendation, condemnation, and consummation.

A. *The Word Commended.* ". . . Moses' seat . . . observe and do . . . ."

Jesus never took one jot or tittle from the Old Testament, the Bible of His day. It was binding; it was good. Higher critics may seek to separate the chaff (?) from the wheat. But Jesus never questioned one word of this recorded revelation of God. Note His repeated quotations from it.

This revelation of God is basic in the moral structure of the universe. Note the Ten Commandments. They are not right because they are in the Decalogue. They are there because they are right. No man or group of men can ignore God's Word without paying the penalty.

Jesus said, "All therefore whatsoever they bid you observe, that observe and do." "Observe" means to take note of it as to its intrinsic value. "Do" means to make obedience to it the habit of one's practice. Jesus commends both right teaching and right practice insofar as God's Word is concerned.

B. *The Deed Condemned.* ". . . do not after their works . . . they say, and do not."

"They keep on saying, and they keep on not doing." Jesus condemns such. *Orthodoxy* and *orthopraxy* should go hand in hand (cf. James 2:10-20).

What did Jesus condemn in the Pharisees? (1) A dog in the manger attitude (23:13). (2) Purposeless enthusiasm unto evil results (23:15). (3) Rote rules which evade essential Christian character (23:16-22; cf. Exod. 20:7; Matt. 5:33-37). (4) A meticulous letter-of-the-law attitude which ignores the true spiritual meaning (23:23-24). (5) Outward honesty but inward "extortion" (robbery) and "excess" (greed) (23:25-26). (6) Outward purity and inward impurity (23:27-28). (7) Abhorring the sins of others while practicing greater sins in God's sight (23:29-33). Note that these were the sins of the religious leaders of Jesus' day. Everyone who aspires to deal with sacred things should beware!

C. *The Result Consummated.* ". . . your house is left unto you desolate."

Here is cause and effect. It is the verdict of history, of
eternity. Jesus saw the holocaust of A.D. 70. But more, He
recognized the present tragedy (cf. Rev. 3:1). The nation and
its leaders had proved their refusal to be used of God. So
only this judgment remained. God went away from Israel to
build a people who at that time was not a people (cf. Hosea
1:6; I Peter 2:9-10). God was not inextricably bound to one
nation or people then. Nor is He now. The judgment of Matthew 23 has been repeated often. It may be again and again.

If this judgment applies to nations, it includes individual
persons also. God has commended His Word. He condemns
its abuse. The same result may be consummated in a man as
in a nation. The word "hell" in verse 33 is "Gehenna," Jesus'
word for the place of eternal punishment. No hell, some say?
Whose word will one follow? The critics or the Christ?

Matthew 24

THE SECOND COMING OF CHRIST

24:3. "And as he sat upon the mount of Olives, the disciples came unto him privately, saying, Tell us, when shall these things be? and what shall be the sign of thy coming, and of the end of the world?"

24:4. "And Jesus answered and said unto them, Take heed that no man deceive you."

I. HISTORICAL SETTING. This was late afternoon on Tuesday of Passion Week. The "day of controversy" was over. Jesus and the Twelve had left Jerusalem, and were on their way to Bethany. Passing through the temple area the Twelve had pointed out to Jesus the magnificence of the temple. Jesus, in turn, prophesied its destruction which came in A.D. 70 at the end of the Jewish War (A.D. 66-70). Probably stopping to rest somewhere on the Mount of Olives, the Twelve (Mark 13:3 identifies Peter, Andrew, James, and John) came to Jesus with three questions: the destruction of Jerusalem; the second coming; and the end of the world. Matthew 24-25 is the answer to these questions. It is difficult to follow these answers, for Jesus dealt with first one and then another. This is the most difficult passage in the Synoptic Gospels. But a clear picture may be discerned if one keeps the three questions in mind. It is well to remember that Jesus is using apocalyptic language which relied upon imagery to express prosaic truth.

II. EXPOSITORY MEANING

Matt. 24:3. "when shall these things be?" This question refers to the destruction of Jerusalem and the temple which occurred in A.D. 70. "Coming." This translates a Greek word *parousia,* used in the papyri of the visit of an emperor. Literally it means "presence." It is used in the Gospels only here and in Matthew 24:27, 37, 39, but is found often in the Epistles (cf. Phil. 2:12; II Thess. 2:1). "The end of the world." Literally, "the consummation of the age." Like *parousia* this phrase occurs in the Gospels only in Matthew. In the New Testament these were technical terms for the second coming of Christ.

Matt. 24:4. "take heed." This Greek verb could be either an indicative or an imperative, probably the latter here. "Deceive" means to lead astray or cause to wander. This warning runs through the entire discourse. It was needed then. It is needed now.

III. DOCTRINAL VALUE. This passage involves the second coming of Christ. It also deals with the destruction of Jerusalem. The warning as to false messiahs and as to misinterpretation of world events is quite evident. The refrain running throughout is that of readiness for the return of the Lord.

IV. PRACTICAL AIM. To seek to interpret Jesus' great discourse in the light of the questions posed by the disciples. Extreme and dogmatic positions should be avoided. Jesus set no timetable of events, nor should anyone else. The fact He declared. That is sufficient. The time element should be left with God. Readiness is the key throughout — for one's self (24:44) and for the whole world (24:14).

V. HOMILETICAL FORM
Theme: "The Second Coming of Christ."

Introduction: No words of Jesus have been subjected to a more careful scrutiny. Nor have any others been the basis of a greater diversity of interpretation. But the "blessed hope" inspires students of God's Word to seek their teaching. Only as one keeps in mind the three specific questions which Jesus answered may one hope to approximate the meaning of Jesus' words. Three words may help in revealing the content of this passage: warning, description, and declaration.

A. *The Warning of Jesus.* "Take heed that no man deceive you."

This is a needed caution. Jesus foresaw the pandemonium

which would accompany this "blessed hope." It is obvious that Jesus had in mind at this point all three questions. Note the warnings. (1) As to false Christs (24:5). This relates to all three questions. False Christs abounded just prior to and during the Jewish War (A.D. 66-70). They have continued through the ages. (2) As to cataclysmic world events (24:6-7). But these are not a sign of the *Parousia*. They are parts of world history. (3) As to persecution (24:8-13). "The beginning of sorrows" refers to the persecution of Christians, not to the approaching end of the age. This began in widespread scope about A.D. 66-70 as a policy of the Roman Empire. (4) The one sure sign (24:14). Through tribulation the gospel will be spread through the ages until the end of the age.

This warning is needed today. False messiahs have dotted the pages of history. Political, economic, philosophical, theological, and theosophical messiahs repeatedly present themselves. Note modern cults. Jesus said, "Do not go after them" (24:23-26). Every great disturbance among governments, in nature, and in society produces its cries, "The end is near." But life goes on.

B. *The Description by Jesus.* "When shall these things be?" Matthew 24:15-22 answers this first question. The "abomination of desolation" refers to the fall of Jerusalem. "Abomination" refers to a nausea caused by a stench. Idolatry is described as a stench in God's nostrils. When Jerusalem fell the Romans offered heathen sacrifices at the eastern gate of the city near the temple area.

Note Jesus' warnings in this regard. "Get out of Jerusalem when you see the armies gathering" (cf. Luke 21:20 ff.). Eusebius says that at that time many Christians fled to Pella, a town in the mountains about seventeen miles south of the sea of Galilee. Those with child or nursing children could not run. Winter would produce added hardships. A sabbath day's journey would not allow them to escape. Had the carnage of the fall of the nation continued, no one would have escaped. For the Christians' sake God shortened the days of it.

Such an experience would produce false messiahs and prophets. Ignore them. When the Christ appears all will see Him (24:27). To Him His own will gather (24:28).

This is Jesus' prophecy of what today is recorded history. It serves as a warning to all ages, including ours, not to be deceived by world events about us. This does not mean that His *Parousia* is not near. It is always imminent. Modern man's responsibility is not to chart events and fix speculative dates. He is to be ready, and busy getting others ready (24:14).

C. *The Declaration of Jesus.* "... the sign of thy coming ... the end of the world."

Verse 29 ff. deals with these questions. Verses 29-31 are apocalyptic language commonly used in connection with the coming of the Christ or of some other cataclysmic intervention of God in history. The sign? "The Son of man in heaven" or in the sky (24:30). Those unprepared will mourn. His own will rejoice (24:31). "This generation" probably refers to the destruction of Jerusalem, a literal fact. In just forty years it occurred. "But the day and the hour" of the second coming is known only to God (24:36). There it should remain. Life will go on its way until the end (24:37-39). Some will be ready, others will not be (24:39-41). But Christian people are to "watch" in service (24:42). Lost people are to prepare through faith in Christ (24:43). "Therefore be ye also ready: for in such an hour as ye think not the Son of man cometh" (24:44).

Matthew 25

THE INTERIM RESPONSIBILITY

25:14. "For the kingdom of heaven is as a man travelling into a far country, who called his own servants, and delivered unto them his goods."

25:19. "After a long time the Lord of those servants cometh, and reckoneth with them."

25:29. "For unto every one that hath shall be given, and he shall have abundance: but from him that hath not shall be taken away even that which he hath."

I. HISTORICAL SETTING. The scene is the same as in Chapter 24. With a series of parables (24:45—25:46) Jesus points out various aspects of the time between His ascension and second coming. The import of all is that in the Lord's return character will be revealed and rewarded or condemned accordingly.

II. EXPOSITORY MEANING
Matt. 25:14. Literally, "For as a man travelling into a far country called his own servants . . . ." "Travelling into a far country." This is one word, a participle, meaning to be away from one's home or country. He was about to go abroad. Note Jesus' ascension, etc. "His own servants" or slaves. This corresponds to Jesus' own followers. Paul called himself a slave of Jesus Christ (cf. Gal. 1:10). "Goods" are "belongings," all that he had of earthly goods.
Matt. 25:19. "After a long time" or much time. Note that no date is specified. This suggests a delay. "Reckoneth." Two Greek papyri and one ostracon have this as a business idiom. Literally, "He makes a reckoning."
Matt. 25:29. Literally, "For to the one having, all things shall be given, and he shall be overflowing all the edges

around [as a bowl overflows which cannot contain its contents]; but from the one not having, even what he has shall be taken away from him." Opportunity used and rewarded; opportunity neglected and lost.

III. DOCTRINAL VALUE. This is a lesson in stewardship, not merely of money, but of the Christian life and its opportunities. God has placed Kingdom affairs in the hands of His people. He will demand a reckoning upon His return. Ability and faithfulness, not results, will be the determining factors in judgment. One's fruits prove the true Christian character or lack of it.

IV. PRACTICAL AIM. To bring each person face to face with his responsibility as a Christian. Each has the same opportunity. Not all give the same response. God does not look for excuses but results. Fruitless church members may well question their Christian experience.

V. HOMILETICAL FORM

Theme: "The Interim Responsibility."

Introduction: In the crucifixion and resurrection God completed His work of redemption. Henceforth, under the guidance of the Holy Spirit, He will propagate it among men. Jesus is going away, and will some day return. What of the interim? This is the burden of the parable of the talents. Its message may be described as bestowal, reckoning, and reward.

A. *The Bestowal of Responsibility*. ". . . delivered unto them his goods."

Five, two, one "to every man according to his several ability." "His own servants" refers to each Christian individually and to the Church collectively. He has committed to His people the things of the Kingdom, His revelation of God and man, His redemptive work, His call to repentance, His gospel, the "power of God unto salvation to every one that believeth." To each Christian He has committed according to his ability. Happily, some are faithful. Sadly, some are untrustworthy. They waste their Master's goods. Are these latter Christians at all (cf. Matt. 7:16-29)?

B. *The Reckoning.* ". . . reckoneth with them."

Those who propose to do business for God have business with God. Responsibility is not bestowed by God and then forgotten.

Note that each of the first two servants reported the same increase. They doubled that which was entrusted to them. God holds man responsible for what he has, not what he has not (cf. II Cor. 8:12). Success is determined by endowment. He does not demand an "A" out of a "B" student. Nor is He satisfied with a "B" from an "A" student. A Church or a Christian is judged by its faithfulness to opportunity.

Note further the third servant. He is not condemned for not producing, but for not trying. Jesus condemned him with his own words (25:24-27). He had not wasted his master's goods. He had buried them. Fear became his master, not Jesus. He served out of fear, not love.

The reports of the servants are most revealing. The first two used sixteen words to report their successes. The third needed forty-three words to explain or alibi his failure. God is not interested in excuses but in results. This applies to churches as well as individuals.

C. *The Reward.* ". . . good and faithful . . . wicked and slothful . . . ."

One should never belittle the matter of rewards as a Christian incentive. Jesus magnified them repeatedly. There are degrees of reward in heaven as there are degrees of punishment in hell (cf. I Cor. 3:8, 14-15; Luke 12:47-48).

Note that the first two servants received the same reward. The same is true of churches and individuals. In God's sight there are no little churches and big churches, or little Christians and big Christians. Each is little or big as it chooses to be. God recognizes the result.

The third servant lost what he had. It is a law of life. Note "wicked and slothful." Laziness is wickedness in God's sight. Not only did he lose his opportunity. He lost his soul (25:30). He was "unprofitable." This word means "garbage" (cf. Rom. 3:12, verb form of noun "unprofitable" in 25:30). He was fit only for the garbage dump (cf. Gehenna, hell). This does not mean falling from grace. He was never in grace. His "wicked and lazy" attitude only proved the true character which he had (cf. Matt. 25:31-46). One may question as to whether the third was a Christian.

Those who claim to follow Christ should beware of mere lip service (cf. Matt. 7:21-23). Works alone do not save. But works, or their lack, do declare the quality of faith which does save (cf. James 2:14-20). If one is faithful in his opportunity, God will see to the results.

Matthew 26

A STUDY IN LIGHT AND SHADOWS

26:7. "There came unto him a woman having an alabaster box of very precious ointment, and poured it on his head, as he sat at meat."

26:8. "But when his disciples saw it, they had indignation, saying, To what purpose is this waste?"

26:15. "And said unto them, What will ye give me, and I will deliver him unto you? And they covenanted with him for thirty pieces of silver."

I. HISTORICAL SETTING. This event took place on Tuesday night in Bethany at the home of Simon the leper. After a hard day Jesus was the guest of a friend, maybe one whom He had healed of leprosy. According to John Lazarus was present. Martha served. The anointing was done by Mary (John 12:1-3). The disciples complained of Mary's "waste." John notes that Judas did this. Probably the others joined in. Some identify this event with Luke 7:36 ff. But the differences between the events are quite evident. There is no reason why both could not have happened. Note that John supplies details omitted by Mark and Matthew. When he wrote the characters probably were dead, and so could be named with impunity. John identifies the woman whose good deed became a memorial to her. He also shows the immediate reason for Judas' betrayal (cf. John 12:4; Matt. 26:14-16).

II. EXPOSITORY MEANING
Matt. 26:7. "woman." John identifies her as Mary of Bethany (John 12:3). "An alabaster box of very precious ointment." This flask got its name from the town in Egypt where the material was found. It was used to contain precious ointments. The ointment was "exceeding precious," of weighty

121

value or a great price. "An alabaster of nard (*murou*) was a present for a king" (Bruce). Herodotus lists it as one of five presents sent by Cambyses to the King of Ethiopia. "Poured it on his head." Literally, "poured down." John says that she "anointed the feet of Jesus." She did both in a great act of love.

Matt. 26: 8. "disciples." John singles out Judas as the leader in this complaint (John 12:4). "Waste." Literally, "a total loss." Just so much "sentimental aroma" (Robertson). "She was a poet and they were somewhat prosaic" (Bruce).

Matt. 26:15. "give me." Literally, "what do you will to me to give." Their price, not his. Note the contrast between Mary and Judas. "And I" is one word (*kagō*). "I," even one of His disciples. "Deliver." This means to hand over (cf. Matt. 27:26 b.). "Covenanted." Literally, "they weighed" as in balances. "Coined money was in use, but the shekels may have been weighed out in antique fashion by men careful to do an iniquitous thing in the most orthodox way" (Bruce). "thirty pieces of silver" (cf. Zech. 11:12). Less than twenty-five dollars, the current price of a slave.

III. DOCTRINAL VALUE. This incident shows the different reactions to Jesus, love and hate. Spiritual deeds are a waste to unspiritual people. Virtue has its reward. Note the final disastrous end to wrong spiritual attitudes. Judas' deed was not one of passionate anger but of calculated greed.

IV. PRACTICAL AIM. To show the outward fruit of inward attitudes. Love will find a way. The love of money is the root of every kind of evil. Profit and loss cannot be measured by man's balances but by God's.

V. HOMILETICAL FORM.
  Theme: "A Study in Light and Shadows."
Introduction: The deed of Mary was an island of love in a sea of hate. It was a ray of light shining through the lowering clouds of the storm which was about to burst upon Jesus (26:2-5). The result is one of the most meaningful stories in the life of our Lord. It is all the more so since it is painted

against the ugly background of greed and hatred. This scene may be described as realization, reaction, and result.

A. *The Realization.* "...a woman...his disciples...."

In all probability Mary and Judas were the first of Jesus' disciples fully to realize that He was going to the cross. Jesus' announcement (26:2) made it certain. Possibly Judas even knew about the meeting of the Sanhedrin (26:3-5).

Neither could prevent the crucifixion. Upon realizing that the end was near, each asked a question. Mary: "What can I do for Jesus?" Judas: "What can Jesus do for me?" Why this difference? Each had had equal opportunities to know the innermost heart of Jesus. But with far different results. The one was a true believer. The other was merely a *joiner* for selfish reasons. He was an unregenerated devil (cf. John 6:70-71).

In any generation those gathered about Jesus may be divided into the Marys and the Judases. One is Christ-centered. The other is self-centered. One asks, "What may I do?" The other asks, "What must I do?" The one asks, "What service may I render?" The other asks, "What is there in it for me?" Through the one Christ is glorified. Through the other He is crucified .

B. *The Reaction.* ". . . very precious ointment . . . this waste."

Mary's answer was sympathetic love and understanding. She did what she could to alleviate His suffering. She gave to Him her very best. It was her gift to the King.

Judas' answer was carping criticism of her act. He despised Mary because he despised Jesus. Note how his act even contaminated the very elect (disciples). If Mary eased the heart of Jesus, Judas broke it. Note further that his criticism of Mary was intended to cover up his own sin of thievery (cf. John 12:6). Under the hypocritical guise of charity he sought to further his own gains. Trouble makers in the church usually have an ulterior motive. They may fool the disciples, but not the Lord. Crass materialism always regards spiritual investments as "waste," a waste of time and money. But the Lord accepts it as a gracious and eternal service (26:10-13).

C. *The Result.* "a memorial unto her . . . what will ye give me . . . ."

Mary's was a selfless act, but it redounded to her eternal glory. Judas' was a selfish deed, but it brought to him eternal shame. Mary received that which she did not seek. Judas lost that which he sought (cf. Matt. 27:3-10), even his life (cf. Matt. 27:5), yea, his soul.

Judas sold out too cheaply. Note that the Sanhedrin set the price (Matt. 26:15a). "The wages of sin is death . . ." (Rom. 6:23). The devil drives a hard bargain.

Through the centuries Mary's name is breathed with reverence. Judas' name is uttered with a curse. Men name their lovely daughters after Mary. They do not even name their dogs after Judas. The only thing named Judas is the goat which leads sheep to the slaughter. Mary's timeless monument is the preaching of the living Word. Judas' name adorns a potter's cemetery. Amen.

Matthew 27

THE KING ON TRIAL

27:11. "And Jesus stood before the governor: and the governor asked him, saying, Art thou the King of the Jews? And Jesus said unto him, Thou sayest."

27:17. "Therefore when they were gathered together, Pilate said unto them, Whom will ye that I release unto you? Barabbas, or Jesus which is called Christ?"

27:22. "Pilate saith unto them, What shall I do then with Jesus which is called Christ? They all say unto him, Let him be crucified."

I. HISTORICAL SETTING. It is early Friday morning in Jerusalem. Shortly after midnight Jesus was arrested by the temple police, and brought before Annas. Annas was a former high priest who still ran the office through his son-in-law Caiaphas. The Jewish trial comprised three parts: (1) preliminary examination before Annas (John 18:12-14, 19-23); (2) informal pre-dawn trial by the Sanhedrin (Matt. 26:57, 59-68 and parallels in Mark, Luke, and John); (3) formal condemnation before the Sanhedrin (Matt. 27:1; Mark 15:1; Luke 22:66-71). By Jewish law it was illegal on most every count.

Since the Sanhedrin could not pronounce the death sentence, they brought Jesus to Pilate, the Roman Governor. Here again the trial may be divided into three phases: (1) before Pilate the first time (Matt. 27:2, 11-14 and parallels in the other three Gospels. John 18:28-38 gives the most details here); before Herod Antipas (Luke 23:6-12); before Pilate the second time (Matt. 27:15-26 and parallels. Again John furnishes the longer account). Despite the Roman pride for justice, here again many illegalities are found.

Matthew's account involves parts of both appearances before Pilate. For convenience it may be treated as one. Jesus is still in control as He proceeds to die as a King.

II. EXPOSITORY MEANING

Matt. 27:11. "governor." Pilate, the Roman provincial governor. He was a *legatus Caesaris* or procurator who ruled over one of the lesser provinces. "Art thou the King of the Jews?" Literally, "You are the King of the Jews?" The Sanhedrin had so charged that He made this claim. Note their subtlety in giving "Christ" a political connotation (cf. Luke 23:2). Pilate's question invited an affirmative answer. "Thou sayest." Jesus turns the answer on this thought. Jesus confessed that He was their King (cf. John 18:36-37). The Jews had charged Jesus with this claim (cf. Luke 23:2-3), but gave it a political flavor. Note that Jesus did not reply to the Jews. Nor did He do so to the direct questioning of Pilate. Note Matthew 27:14. Literally, "He did not answer to him up to even one word." Jesus had established His Kingship. That was all that He wanted.

Matt. 27:17. "gathered together." They were now before Pilate the second time. "Will ye." A choice of the will, not a passing desire. "Release." This custom (cf. 27:15) is mentioned only here and in Josephus (Ant. XX. 9, 3). "Barabbas." This means in Aramaic "son of father." Mark 15:7 describes him as an insurrectionist and a murderer. The very kind of messiah which Jesus refused to be. Some manuscripts call him "Jesus Barabbas." Note the sharp contrast with "Jesus the one being called Christ" (literal reading).

III. DOCTRINAL VALUE. The doctrine which runs through this passage is that of the Kingship of Jesus Christ. Pilate thought that he sat in judgment upon Jesus. The opposite was true. Cowardice still allows Jesus to be crucified. Men still choose Barabbas and crucify Jesus. Wrong may be on the throne, but not forever.

IV. PRACTICAL AIM. To see in the trial of Jesus the trial of every man. God offers alternatives, but man must live and/or die with his choice. Through all the shouts of greed and hate Jesus still reigns as King.

V. HOMILETICAL FORM

Theme: "The King On Trial."

Introduction: This is one of the most dramatic moments in history. The King of kings standing before the rulers of earth. It is also one of the most sordid scenes. For here the legal justice of both Jew and Gentile stands condemned. History records that Jesus was on trial before them. But the final verdict of history records that they were on trial before Him. The one is convicted of venomous pre-judgment. The other stands condemned of cowardly surrender to material opportunism. Justice has often been nailed to a cross for such reasons. So the courtroom in Pilate's hall blends into the halls of history where wrong upon the throne has repeatedly nailed truth to the scaffold. The timely and timeless lesson is revealed as conviction, choice, and consequence.

A. *The Conviction.* "You are the King of the Jews?" (literal translation).

Jesus' answer turned the tables on Pilate. Whether he actually believed Jesus to be a King may be open to question. But there is solid evidence that he suspected as much (cf. Matt. 27:19; John 18:33-38). Certainly he judged Jesus as innocent of political charges. Jesus' Kingdom was in the realm of truth. Pilate's references to Jesus as a King were scorn for the Jews, but there could have been more. As in the mockery of the soldiers (Matt. 27:28-29), so here, God causes the wrath of man to praise Him.

Jesus stands before every man as a King. Some may deny it for various reasons: Sanhedrin (prejudice); multitudes (indifference); Pilate (moral cowardice); soldiers (spiritual hardness). Finite minds put Jesus on trial, but the ages have vindicated Him. The burden of proof is upon him who would question the Kingship of Jesus. The time will come when every knee shall bow, and every tongue shall confess Him as Lord (cf. Phil. 2:11).

B. *The Choice.* "... Barabbas, or Jesus ...?"

The choice was greater than any of the choosers realized. Origen reports having seen a manuscript of Matthew's Gospel wherein Barabbas is called "Jesus Barabbas." This heightens the contrast. "Jesus son of father" versus "Jesus the Son of His Father." "Jesus" means "Jehovah is salvation." Jesus Barabbas offered political salvation. Jesus Christ offered spiritual salvation. The one proposed insurrection. The other promised regeneration. The former offered the nation political freedom through the shedding of their blood. The latter proffered spiritual freedom through the shedding of His own blood. The one would establish a kingdom among men. The other came to establish the Kingdom of God within men.

The multitudes, spurred on by selfish leaders, chose Barabbas and rejected Jesus. They chose the material over the spiritual. Thus Barabbas was turned loose to pursue his evil ways. Jesus was nailed to a cross. Pilate's question is the question of all (cf. Matt. 27:22). He had Jesus on his hands. An analysis of the trial indicates his many efforts to dispose of him: ignore him (John 18:31); praise Him (Luke 23:4); shift responsibility to another (Luke 23:6-12); substitute another (Matt. 27:21); wash his hands of the whole matter (Matt. 27:24). But he still had Jesus on his hands — and on his soul. Men still make the same attempts with the same results. Still the question remains. "What shall I do then with Jesus which is called Christ?"

C. *The Consequence.* ". . . crucified."

This was the cry of the multitude incited by the Sanhedrin. Where were the "Hosannas?" Where were the friends of Jesus? Fled or following afar off. Many who cried "hosanna" on Sunday cried "crucify" on Friday. The fickle nature of popular acclaim!

Who crucified Jesus? Pilate, the Sanhedrin, the soldiers, the multitude? The story is told by the superscription over the cross. Roman law required this. "JESUS OF NAZARETH, THE KING OF THE JEWS" (John 19:19). John notes that it was written in Hebrew (language of religion), Latin (language of government), and Greek (language of culture). These represented the great divisions of people of the Empire. Institutional religion condemned Jesus. Governmental power crucified Him. Pagan culture rejected Him. There is guilt enough for all (cf. Matt. 27:25). There were crucifiers

then — there are crucifiers now. All stand in judgment before
God (cf. Luke 23:28-31).

"Men, brethren, what shall we do?" (Acts 2:37; literal
translation). "Repent..." (Acts 2:38).

Matthew 28

THE COMMISSION OF THE KING

28:18. "And Jesus came and spake unto them, saying, All power is given unto me in heaven and in earth."

28:19. "Go ye therefore, and teach all nations, baptizing them in the name of the Father, and of the Son, and of the Holy Ghost."

28:20. "Teaching them to observe all things whatsoever I have commanded you: and, lo, I am with you alway, even unto the end of the world."

I. HISTORICAL SETTING. The Gospel of Matthew ends in a blaze of glory. In compliance with Jesus' instructions the Eleven came to a mountain in Galilee. Along the way others joined them so that above five hundred were assembled there (cf. I Cor. 15:6). The mountain is not specified. Was it the same one on which Jesus delivered His "Manifesto" (cf. Matt. 5-7)? It is an intriguing thought. At any rate sometime during the forty days between the resurrection and the ascension the event took place. Matthew does not record the ascension, but closes his Gospel with the Great Commission. It is a fitting finale. Here the King looks at all the world and down all ages to the end of the age. Satan had proposed his method of taking the world. Here Jesus gives His plan. The King goes forth to claim His Kingdom.

II. EXPOSITORY MEANING
Matt. 28:18. "All power." The word "power" translates a word meaning "out of being." It means *authority* springing from the nature of one's being. "Is given." This is a timeless aorist tense encompassing all future time. "Me." The risen Christ, "Heaven .... earth." Cosmic, absolute power, enhancing "all power."

131

Matt. 28:19. "Go." This is a participle, not an imperative. Literally, "going" or "as you go." "Teach." This is the only imperative in the Commission. It means "make disciples" or "disciple." This is suggestive of the new birth (cf. Matt. 11:29). "All nations." Both Jews and Gentiles. "Baptizing." This is another participle. After *discipling* comes baptism. "Name." This refers to authority. "Father ... Son ... Holy Ghost" [Spirit]. Not trine immersion, but one, in the name of the Trinity.

Matt. 28:20. "teaching." This is a different word from "teach" in verse 19. It refers to the process of instruction after the new birth and baptism. "Observe" means to practice. "I am with you." "I" is stated, and so emphatic. "I, the risen Christ, am with you." "Always" or "all the days," suggesting a long period of time. "The end of the world." Literally, "The consummation of the age."

III. DOCTRINAL VALUE. The doctrine taught here is missions or evangelism in its larger sense. It includes the new birth, but also involves baptism, and growth in grace, knowledge, and service, or sanctification. The presence of Christ in the interim and His second advent are clearly set forth. "The consummation of the age" suggests also glorification.

IV. PRACTICAL AIM. To set forth the duty imposed upon all Christians, and the means of fulfilling that duty. Evangelism does not end with conversion or baptism. It extends throughout one's life and through every generation. The evangel does not strive alone, but is assured of the presence and power of the King through His Spirit.

V. HOMILETICAL FORM
Theme: "The Commission of the King."

Introduction: The work of God in Christ for man's redemption is finished. Henceforth it rests with His people as they strive in the power of the Holy Spirit. The King sends forth His emissaries. No script writer would have the audacity to reproduce this scene. A band of peasants with no worldly authority, treasure, or army pitted against the might of a pagan world. Yet history records that in less than three hundred years, they so succeeded that the emperor of that world found it politically expedient to espouse their cause. Whence came this achievement? The answer may be seen in three words: Person, program, and presence.

A. *The Person of the King.* "All power is given unto me . . . ."

It is the risen Christ speaking. He is King in fact as well as in name. The word "power" means "out of the nature of being." So as the Risen Christ, out of that very nature, He commands. What a sublime picture! He sends the five hundred forth in world conquest armed only with spiritual weapons. "According to the spirit of holiness" (Rom. 1:4) He had conquered. He sends them to do the same in the same Spirit. And, what is even more remarkable, He convinced them that they could do it!

The Risen Christ still stands upon every mountain and before every "five hundred." In His authority they have crossed seas, stormed the citadels of sin, and changed the course of the rivers of history. Pagan cultures still defy Him. But King Jesus has never been driven from the field. The arena of battle is the hearts of men. They do not fall before carnal weapons. But they do succumb to the Sword of the Spirit. The battle has been joined, and must be pressed until the flag of the King flutters in the breeze above every heart, every nation. It may be in joyful surrender, or it may be in coerced submission. But "He must reign, till he hath put all enemies under his feet" (I Cor. 15:25). He is reigning now in His mediatorial Kingdom. He will reign supreme in all of eternity.

B. *The Program of the King.* "Go . . . disciple . . . baptizing . . . teaching . . . ."

The King did not leave His work to chance. He spelled out the details. He did not even imply that His people would not go. Hence no command to do so. "Going" or "as ye go . . . ." Then the command. "Disciple all nations." They were to go purposefully. Plant the flag of the King in their hearts. "Baptizing." Lead them to an open declaration of allegiance to Him. "Teaching." To the end that they may become obedient, useful citizens of the Kingdom.

Tragic is the result of ignoring this program: unregenerate church members; *mavericks* with no brand, no local church or denominational allegiance; idle, untrained, useless Christians. Evangelism is more than winning a person to Christ. It does not end with conversion any more than a full life ends with birth. It is only the beginning. Enrolling as a pupil is the beginning not the end. True evangelism involves regeneration, sanctification, and glorification. All are found in the Great Commission.

C. *The Presence of the King.* "I am with you . . . ."

This is Matthew's equivalent of John 14-16. For the King spoke not of bodily but of spiritual presence. "With you" in power, guidance, comfort, courage, understanding, and victory. The disciples needed this promise. And they found it fulfilled times without number.

Men often express the wish that they might have been with Jesus in bodily presence when He walked the earth. But the modern Christian has more. Then Jesus was *with* them. Now He is *in* them. Then He was in only one place at one time. Now He is omnipresent. Then He was present only for a few years. Now "I am with you alway, even unto the end of the world."

BIBLIOGRAPHY

The Expositor's Greek Testament, Vol. I, "The Gospel According to Matthew," A. B. Bruce, Eerdmans, Grand Rapids, 1951.

A. T. Robertson, *Word Pictures in the Greek New Testament,* Vol. I, Sunday School Board of the Southern Baptist Convention, Nashville, 1930.

-----, *A Harmony of the Gospels,* Broadman, Nashville, 1950.

Matthew Henry, *A Commentary on the Whole Bible,* Vol. V, Revell, New York.

Alfred Edersheim, *The Life and Times of Jesus the Messiah,* Vol. I and II, Eerdmans, Grand Rapids, 1953.

John A. Broadus, *Commentary on the Gospel of Matthew,* American Baptist Publication Society, Philadelphia, 1886.

G. Campbell Morgan, *The Crises of the Christ,* Revell, New York, 1936.

-----, *The Parables and Metaphors of our Lord,* Revell, New York, 1943.

-----, *The Gospel of Matthew,* Revell, New York, 1929.

J. W. Shepard, *The Christ of the Gospels,* Eerdmans, Grand Rapids, 1947.

John Peter Lange, *The Life of the Lord Jesus,* Vols. I-IV, Zondervan, Grand Rapids, 1958.

Charles H. Spurgeon, *Sermons on the Parables,* Zondervan, Grand Rapids, 1958.

-----, *Sermons on the Miracles,* Zondervan, Grand Rapids, 1958.

The International Standard Bible Encyclopaedia, Vols. I-V, Eerdmans, Grand Rapids, 1949.

DATE DUE

FEB 20   NOV 1 0   NOV 2 3 1997

JAN 25   NOV 1 2

APR 22   MAY 1 6 2002

MAR 19 NOV 2 4   AUG 0 8 2001

DEC 8

MAR 8

MAR 22   FEB 20 NOV 0 9 2009

APR 18   JAN 2

DEC 15   Apr 16 OCT 1 4 2012

AUG 2

NOV 11   NOV 28

FEB 12

MAR 4   DEC 2

MAR 1 1 MAY 2 1 '87

MAY 20   DEC 21 1988

NOV 23 FEB 18 '89

DEC 8

MAR 3 0 NOV 23 1989

MAY 1 1 JUL. 2 0 1990

'UL 2 9'